ANCIENT WISDOM

Modern World Advice
For Better Living from
Sages Through the Ages:
The Philosophers
Handbook

Gopi Vishnu, Ph.D

NMD Books
Simi Valley, CA

Ancient Wisdom: Modern World - Advice For Better Living
From Sages Through the Ages
by Gopi Vishnu, Ph.D

Visit our Web site at http://www.NMDbooks.com.

Library of Congress Control Number: 2011924057

ISBN: 978-1-936828-13-5   (Softcover)

First Edition January 2011

Introduction

Throughout time, man has pondered the meaning of life and his purpose. He has puzzled and ruminated, agonized and speculated, and sometimes he has found answers - only to come up short and to continue back to the beginning of the inquiry again.

Such questions have been pondered for many centuries, and through those centuries a great many sages and scribes, philosophers, dreamers and doers have left us with a vast storehouse of information.

This storehouse contains the writings of the wise men of many generations past; many of whom felt they found the answer to the question of life and its many challenges.

To find the great answers of the riddles of life one need only to reach out to hear the voices from the past. The ancient men speak even now through their timeless words.

Through the many years of my studies as both a teacher of Philosophy and as a researcher in the fields of psychology and sociology, I have come to rely on the advice of these ancient men to help me understand the mysteries and vicissitudes of life, to help me find the peace of mind and inner contentment I seek.

Millions of others have also come to find solace and guidance in these writings, to help them find a sense of purpose and meaning in their lives.

I decided I would take the best of these and collect them in a book that was compact, easy to read and simple to understand, hence, the work you see before you.

This slim volume is not meant to be a comprehensive compendium of all the greatest philosophic texts ever written, but rather what I feel is s snapshot or one sliver from an essential core of great philosophy that contains within it a small yet mighty kernal of truth.

I offer them here in the hope their words will echo back from centuries past to enlighten and give new hope and meaning to lives both present and future.

One need not say more, the ancient ones speak for themselves.

Gopi Vishnu
Los Angeles
2011

Table of Contents

Aristotle
(384 BC – 322 BC)

Aristotle was a Greek philosopher, a student of Plato and teacher of Alexander the Great. His writings cover many subjects, including physics, metaphysics, poetry, theater, music, logic, rhetoric, linguistics, politics, government, ethics, biology, and zoology.

Together with Plato and Socrates (Plato's teacher), Aristotle is one of the most important founding figures in Western philosophy. Aristotle's writings were the first to create a comprehensive system of Western philosophy, encompassing morality and aesthetics, logic and science, politics and metaphysics.

Aristotle's views on the physical sciences profoundly shaped medieval scholarship, and their influence extended well into the Renaissance, although they were ultimately replaced by Newtonian physics. In the zoological sciences, some of his observations were confirmed to be accurate only in the 19th century.

His works contain the earliest known formal study of logic, which was incorporated in the late 19th century into modern formal logic. In metaphysics, Aristotelianism had a profound influence on philosophical and theological thinking in the Islamic and Jewish traditions in the Middle Ages, and it continues to influence Christian theology, especially the scholastic tradition of the Catholic Church.

His ethics, though always influential, gained renewed interest with the modern advent of virtue ethics. All aspects of Aristotle's philosophy continue to be the object of active academic study today. Though Aristotle wrote many elegant treatises and dialogues (Cicero described his literary style as "a river of gold"), it is thought that the majority of his writings are now lost and only about one-third of the original works have survived.

Excerpt From Aristotle's "Ethics," Book I:

We must now inquire concerning Happiness, not only from our conclusion and the data on which our reasoning proceeds, but likewise from what is commonly said about it: because with what is true all things which really are are in harmony, but with that which is false the true very soon jars.

Now there is a common division of goods into three classes; one being called external, the other two those of the soul and body respectively, and those belonging to the soul we call most properly and specially good.

Well, in our definition we assume that the actions and workings of the soul constitute Happiness, and these of course belong to the soul. And so our account is a good one, at least according to this opinion, which is of ancient date, and accepted by those who profess philosophy.

Rightly too are certain actions and workings said to be the end, for thus it is brought into the number of the goods of the soul instead of the external. Agreeing also with our definition is the common notion, that the happy man lives well and does well, for it has been stated by us to be pretty much a kind of living well and doing well.

But further, the points required in Happiness are found in combination in our account of it.

For some think it is virtue, others practical wisdom, others a kind of scientific philosophy; others that it is these, or else some one of them, in combination with pleasure, or at least not independently of it; while others again take in external prosperity.

Of these opinions, some rest on the authority of numbers or antiquity, others on that of few, and those men of note: and it is not likely that either of these classes should be wrong in all points, but be right at least in some one, or even in most.

Now with those who assert it to be Virtue (Excellence), or some kind of Virtue, our account agrees: for working in the way of Excellence surely belongs to Excellence.

And there is perhaps no unimportant difference between conceiving of the Chief Good as in possession or as in use, in other words, as a mere state or as a working. For the state or habit may possibly exist in a subject without effecting any good, as, for instance, in him who is asleep, or in any other way inactive; but the working cannot so, for it will of necessity act, and act well.

And as at the Olympic games it is not the finest and strongest men who are crowned, but they who enter the lists, for out of these the prize-men are selected; so too in life, of the honourable and the good, it is they who act who rightly win the prizes.

Their life too is in itself pleasant: for the feeling of pleasure is a mental sensation, and that is to each pleasant of which he is said to be fond: a horse, for instance, to him who is fond of horses, and a sight to him who is fond of sights: and so in like manner just acts to him who is fond of justice, and more generally the things in accordance with virtue to him who is fond of virtue.

Now in the case of the multitude of men the things which they individually esteem pleasant clash, because they are not such by nature, whereas to the lovers of nobleness those things are pleasant which are such by nature: but the actions in accordance with virtue are of this kind, so that they are pleasant both to the individuals and also in themselves.

So then their life has no need of pleasure as a kind of additional appendage, but involves pleasure in itself. For, besides what I have just mentioned, a man is not a good man at all who feels no pleasure in noble actions, just as no one would call that man just who does not feel pleasure in acting justly, or liberal who does not in liberal actions, and similarly in the case of the other virtues which might be enumerated: and if this be so, then the actions in accordance with virtue must be in themselves pleasurable.

Then again they are certainly good and noble, and each of these in the highest degree; if we are to take as right the judgment of the good man, for he judges as we have said.

Thus then Happiness is most excellent, most noble, and most pleasant, and these attributes are not separated as in the well-known Delian inscription—

"Most noble is that which is most just, but best is health; And naturally most pleasant is the obtaining one's desires."

For all these co-exist in the best acts of working: and we say that Happiness is these, or one, that is, the best of them.

Still it is quite plain that it does require the addition of external goods, as we have said: because without appliances it is impossible, or at all events not easy, to do noble actions: for friends, money, and political influence are in a manner instruments whereby many things are done: some things there are again a deficiency in which mars blessedness; good birth, for instance, or fine offspring, or even personal beauty: for he is not at all capable of Happiness who is very ugly, or is ill-born, or solitary and childless; and still less perhaps supposing him to have very bad children or friends, or to have lost good ones by death. As we have said already, the addition of prosperity of this kind does seem necessary to complete the idea of Happiness; hence some rank good fortune, and others virtue, with Happiness.

And hence too a question is raised, whether it is a thing that can be learned, or acquired by habituation or discipline of some other kind, or whether it comes in the way of divine dispensation, or even in the way of chance.

Now to be sure, if anything else is a gift of the Gods to men, it is probable that Happiness is a gift of theirs too, and specially because of all human goods it is the highest. But this, it may be, is a question belonging more properly to an investigation different from ours: and it is quite clear, that on the supposition of its not being sent from the Gods direct, but coming to us by reason of virtue and learning of a certain kind, or discipline, it is yet one of the most Godlike things;

because the prize and End of virtue is manifestly somewhat most excellent, nay divine and blessed.

It will also on this supposition be widely participated, for it may through learning and diligence of a certain kind exist in all who have not been maimed for virtue.

And if it is better we should be happy thus than as a result of chance, this is in itself an argument that the case is so; because those things which are in the way of nature, and in like manner of art, and of every cause, and specially the best cause, are by nature in the best way possible: to leave them to chance what is greatest and most noble would be very much out of harmony with all these facts.

The question may be determined also by a reference to our definition of Happiness, that it is a working of the soul in the way of excellence or virtue of a certain kind: and of the other goods, some we must have to begin with, and those which are co-operative and useful are given by nature as instruments.

These considerations will harmonise also with what we said at the commencement: for we assumed the End of [Greek Text: poletikae] to be most excellent: now this bestows most care on making the members of the community of a certain character; good that is and apt to do what is honourable.

With good reason then neither ox nor horse nor any other brute animal do we call happy, for none of them can partake in such working: and for this same reason a child is not happy either, because by reason of his tender age he cannot yet perform such actions: if the term is applied, it is by way of anticipation.

For to constitute Happiness, there must be, as we have said, complete virtue and a complete life: for many changes and chances of all kinds arise during a life, and he who is most prosperous may become involved in great misfortunes in his old age, as in the heroic poems the tale is told of Priam: but the man who has experienced such fortune and died in wretchedness, no man calls happy.

Are we then to call no man happy while he lives, and, as Solon would have us, look to the end? And again, if we are to maintain this position, is a man then happy when he is dead? or is not this a complete absurdity, specially in us who say Happiness is a working of a certain kind?

If on the other hand we do not assert that the dead man is happy, and Solon does not mean this, but only that one would then be safe in pronouncing a man happy, as being thenceforward out of the reach of evils and misfortunes, this too admits of some dispute, since it is thought that the dead has somewhat both of good and evil (if, as we must allow, a man may have when alive but not aware of the circumstances), as honour and dishonour, and good and bad fortune of children and descendants generally.

Nor is this view again without its difficulties: for, after a man has lived in blessedness to old age and died accordingly, many changes may befall him in right of his descendants; some of them may be good and obtain positions in life accordant to their merits, others again quite the contrary: it is plain too that the descendants may at different intervals or grades stand in all manner of relations to the ancestors.

Absurd indeed would be the position that even the dead man is to change about with them and become at one time happy and at another miserable. Absurd however it is on the other hand that the affairs of the descendants should in no degree and during no time affect the ancestors.

But we must revert to the point first raised, since the present question will be easily determined from that.

If then we are to look to the end and then pronounce the man blessed, not as being so but as having been so at some previous time, surely it is absurd that when he is happy the truth is not to be asserted of him, because we are unwilling to pronounce the living happy by reason of their liability to changes, and because, whereas we have conceived of happiness as something stable and no way easily changeable, the fact is that good and bad fortune are constantly circling about the same people: for it is quite plain, that if we are to depend upon the fortunes of men, we shall often have to call the same man happy, and a little while after miserable, thus representing our happy man

"Chameleon-like, and based on rottenness."

Is not this the solution? that to make our sentence dependent on the changes of fortune, is no way right: for not in them stands the well, or the ill, but though human life needs these as accessories (which we have allowed already), the workings in the way of virtue are what determine Happiness, and the contrary the contrary.

And, by the way, the question which has been here discussed, testifies incidentally to the truth of our account of Happiness. For to nothing does a stability of human results attach so much as it does to the workings in the way of virtue, since these are held to be more abiding even than the sciences: and of these last again the most precious are the most abiding, because the blessed live in them most and most continuously, which seems to be the reason why they are not forgotten.

So then this stability which is sought will be in the happy man, and he will be such through life, since always, or most of all, he will be doing and contemplating the things which are in the way of virtue: and the various chances of life he will bear most nobly, and at all times and in all ways harmoniously, since he is the truly good man, or in the terms of our proverb "a faultless cube."

And whereas the incidents of chance are many, and differ in greatness and smallness, the small pieces of good or ill fortune evidently do not affect the balance of life, but the great and numerous, if happening for good, will make life more blessed (for it is their nature to contribute to ornament, and the using of them comes to be noble and excellent), but if for ill, they bruise as it were and maim the blessedness.

For they bring in positive pain, and hinder many acts of working. But still, even in these, nobleness shines through when a man bears contentedly many and great mischances not from insensibility to pain but because he is noble and high-spirited.

And if, as we have said, the acts of working are what determine the character of the life, no one of the blessed can ever become wretched,

13

because he will never do those things which are hateful and mean. For the man who is truly good and sensible bears all fortunes, we presume, becomingly, and always does what is noblest under the circumstances, just as a good general employs to the best advantage the force he has with him; or a good shoemaker makes the handsomest shoe he can out of the leather which has been given him; and all other good artisans likewise.

And if this be so, wretched never can the happy man come to be: I do not mean to say he will be blessed should he fall into fortunes like those of Priam.

Nor, in truth, is he shifting and easily changeable, for on the one hand from his happiness he will not be shaken easily nor by ordinary mischances, but, if at all, by those which are great and numerous; and, on the other, after such mischances he cannot regain his happiness in a little time; but, if at all, in a long and complete period, during which he has made himself master of great and noble things.

Why then should we not call happy the man who works in the way of perfect virtue, and is furnished with external goods sufficient for acting his part in the drama of life: and this during no ordinary period but such as constitutes a complete life as we have been describing it.

Or we must add, that not only is he to live so, but his death must be in keeping with such life, since the future is dark to us, and Happiness we assume to be in every way an end and complete. And, if this be so, we shall call them among the living blessed who have and will have the things specified, but blessed as Men.

On these points then let it suffice to have denned thus much.

Epicurus
(341-270 BC)

Epicurus was an ancient Greek philosopher and the founder of the school of philosophy called Epicureanism. Only a few fragments and letters remain of Epicurus's 300 written works. Much of what is known about Epicurean philosophy derives from later followers and commentators.

For Epicurus, the purpose of philosophy was to attain the happy, tranquil life, characterized by ataraxia, peace and freedom from fear, and aponia, the absence of pain, and by living a self-sufficient life surrounded by friends.

He taught that pleasure and pain are the measures of what is good and evil, that death is the end of the body and the soul and should therefore not be feared, that the gods do not reward or punish humans, that the universe is infinite and eternal, and that events in the world are ultimately based on the motions and interactions of atoms moving in empty space.

Letter to Menoeceus
How to Live a Happy Life

Let no one hesitate to study philosophy while young, and let no one tire of it when old, for it is never too soon nor too late to devote oneself to the well-being of the soul. Whoever says that the time for philosophy has not yet come or that it has already passed is saying that it is too soon or too late for happiness.

Therefore both the young and the old should study philosophy so that, while old, one may still be young with all the joy he has gathered from the past; and while young, one may at the same time be old through fearlessness of the future.

We must practice what produces happiness because when we have it, we have everything, and if we lack it, we shall be doing everything necessary to regain it. So I encourage you, as always, to study and practice my teachings, for they are the basic ingredients of a happy life.

Don't Fear the Gods

A god is an immortal and happy being. This is well-known, but do not believe anything about divine nature other than what is congenial for an eternally happy existence. The gods do exist because we have preconceived notions of them, but they are not like how most people describe them.

Most people embellish their notions of the gods with false beliefs. They credit the gods for delivering rewards and punishments because they commend those who share their own ways and condemn those who do not. Rejecting the popular myths does not make one impious; preaching them is what demonstrates impiety.

Don't Fear Death

Death is no concern to us. All things good and bad are experienced through sensation, but sensation ceases at death. So death is nothing to us, and to know this makes a mortal life happy. Life is not improved by adding infinite time; removing the desire for immortality is what's required. There is no reason why one who is convinced that there is nothing to fear at death should fear anything about it during life.

And whoever says that he dreads death not because it's painful to experience, but only because it's painful to contemplate, is foolish.

It is pointless to agonize over something that brings no trouble when it arrives. So death, the most dreaded of evils, is nothing to us, because when we exist, death is not present, and when death is present, we do not exist. It neither concerns the living nor the dead, since death does not exist for the living, and the dead no longer exist.

Most people, however, either dread death as the greatest of suffering or long for it as a relief from suffering. One who is wise neither renounces life nor fears not living. Life does not offend him, nor does he suppose that not living is any kind of suffering.

16

For just as he would not choose the greatest amount of food over what is most delicious, so too he does not seek the longest possible life, but rather the happiest. And he who advises the young man to live well and the old man to die well is also foolish – not only because it's desirable to live, but because the art of living well and the art of dying well are the same.

And he was still more wrong who said it would be better to have never been born, but that "Once born, be quick to pass through the gates of Hades!" {Theognis, 425 - 427} If he was being serious, why wasn't he himself quick to end his life? Certainly the means were available if this was what he really wanted to do. But if he was not serious, then we have even less reason to believe him.

Future days are neither wholly ours, nor wholly not ours. We must neither depend on them as sure to come nor despair that we won't live to see them.

Master Your Desires

Among desires, some are natural and some are vain. Of those that are natural, some are necessary and some unnecessary. Of those that are necessary, some are necessary for happiness, some for health, and some for life itself. A clear recognition of desires enables one to base every choice and avoidance upon whether it secures or upsets bodily comfort and peace of mind – the goal of a happy life.

Everything we do is for the sake of freedom from pain and anxiety.

Once this is achieved, the storms in the soul are stilled. Nothing else and nothing more are needed to perfect the well-being of the body and soul. It is when we feel pain that we must seek relief, which is pleasure. And when we no longer feel pain, we have all the pleasure we need.

Pleasure, we declare, is the beginning and end of the happy life. We are endowed by nature to recognize pleasure as the greatest good.

Every choice and avoidance we make is guided by pleasure as our standard for judging the goodness of everything.

Although pleasure is the greatest good, not every pleasure is worth choosing. We may instead avoid certain pleasures when, by doing so, we avoid greater pains. We may also choose to accept pain if, by doing so, it results in greater pleasure.

So while every pleasure is naturally good, not every pleasure should be chosen. Likewise, every pain is naturally evil, but not every pain is to be avoided. Only upon considering all consequences should we decide. Thus, sometimes we might regard the good as evil, and conversely: the evil as good.

We regard self-sufficiency as a great virtue – not so that we may only enjoy a few things, but so that we may be satisfied with a few things if those are all we have. We are firmly convinced that those who least yearn for luxury enjoy it most, and that while natural desires are easily fulfilled, vain desires are insatiable.

Plain meals offer the same pleasure as luxurious fare, so long as the pain of hunger is removed. Bread and water offer the greatest pleasure for those in need of them. Accustoming oneself to a simple lifestyle is healthy and it doesn't sap our motivation to perform the necessary tasks of life.

Doing without luxuries for long intervals allows us to better appreciate them and keeps us fearless against changes of fortune. When we say that pleasure is the goal, we do not mean the pleasure of debauchery or sensuality.

Despite whatever may be said by those who misunderstand, disagree with, or deliberately slander our teachings, the goal we do seek is this: freedom from pain in the body and freedom from turmoil in the soul.

For it is not continuous drinking and revelry, the sexual enjoyment of women and boys, or feasting upon fish and fancy cuisine which result in a happy life. Sober reasoning is what is needed, which decides every choice and avoidance and liberates us from the false beliefs which are the greatest source of anxiety.

Live Wisely

The greatest virtue and the basis for all virtues is prudence. Prudence, the art of practical wisdom, is something even more valuable than philosophy, because all other virtues spring from it.

It teaches us that it is not possible to live pleasurably unless one also lives prudently, honorably, and justly; nor is it possible to live prudently, honestly, and justly without living pleasurably. For the virtues are inseparable from a happy life, and living happily is inseparable from the virtues.

Who could conceivably be better off than one who is wise? No one could be more content than one who simply reveres the gods, who is utterly unafraid of death, and who has discovered the natural goal of life.

He understands that pleasure, the greatest good, is easily supplied to absolute fullness, while pain, the greatest evil, lasts only a moment when intense and is easily tolerated when prolonged. Some believe that everything is ruled by fate, but we should dismiss this.

One who is wise knows that the greater power of decision lies within oneself. He understands that while some things are indeed caused by fate, other things happen by chance or by choice. He sees that fate is irreproachable and chance unreliable, but choices deserve either praise or blame because what is decided by choice is not subject to any external power. One would be better off believing in the myths about the gods than to be enslaved by the determinism proclaimed by certain physicists.

At least the myths offer hope of winning divine favors through prayer, but fate can never be appealed. Some believe that chance is a god, but we should dismiss this also. One who is wise knows the gods do not act randomly.

He does not believe that everything is randomly caused.

Nor does he believe, in cases when they are, that chance is doling out good and evil with the intent of making human lives happy or unhappy. He would actually prefer to suffer setbacks while acting wisely than to have miraculous luck while acting foolishly; for it would be better that well-planned actions should perchance fail than ill-planned actions should perchance succeed.

Conclusion

Practice these teachings daily and nightly. Study them on your own or in the company of a like-minded friend, and you shall not be disturbed while awake or asleep. You shall live like a god among men, because one whose life is fortified by immortal blessings in no way resembles a mortal being.

Confucius

(551 BC – 479 BC)

Confucius was a thinker, political figure, educator, and founder of the Ru School of Chinese thought. His teachings, preserved in the Lunyu or Analects, form the foundation of much of subsequent Chinese speculation on the education and comportment of the ideal man, how such an individual should live his live and interact with others, and the forms of society and government in which he should participate. Fung Yu-lan, one of the great 20th century authorities on the history of Chinese thought, compares Confucius' influence in Chinese history with that of Socrates in the West.

"To govern is to correct. If you set an example by being correct, who would dare remain incorrect?"

"He who will not economize will have to agonize."

"When anger rises, think of the consequences."

"It does not matter how slowly you go, so long as you do not stop."

"The superior man is modest in his speech, but excels in his actions."

"The man who moves a mountain begins by carrying away small stones."

"I hear and I forget. I see and I remember. I do and I understand."

"If a man take no thought about what is distant, he will find sorrow near at hand"

"Forget injuries, never forget kindnesses."

"Be not ashamed of mistakes and thus make them crimes."

"To see what is right, and not to do it, is want of courage or of principle."

"The superior man, when resting in safety, does not forget that danger may come. When in a state of security

he does not forget the possibility of ruin. When all is orderly, he does not forget that disorder may come. Thus

his person is not endangered, and his States and all their clans are preserved."

"Respect yourself and others will respect you."

"Ignorance is the night of the mind, but a night without moon and star."

"Study the past if you would define the future."

"What the superior man seeks is in himself; what the small man seeks is in others. "

"Everything has its beauty but not everyone sees it."

"Wheresoever you go, go with all your heart."

"Everything has beauty, but not everyone sees it."

"When we see men of a contrary character, we should turn inwards and examine ourselves."

"It does not matter how slowly you go so long as you do not stop."

"Be not ashamed of mistakes and thus make them crimes. "

"Our greatest glory is not in never falling, but in rising every time we fall."

"Do not be desirous of having things done quickly. Do not look at small advantages. Desire to have things done quickly prevents their being done thoroughly. Looking at small advantages prevents great affairs from being accomplished."

"Our greatest glory is not in never falling, but in rising every time we fall."

"Our greatest glory is not in never falling, but in rising every time we fall."

"I hear and I forget. I see and I remember. I do and I understand."

"The superior man acts before he speaks, and afterwards speaks according to his action."

"I hear and I forget. I see and I believe. I do and I understand."

"By three methods we may learn wisdom: First, by reflection, which is noblest; Second, by imitation, which is easiest; and third by experience, which is the bitterest."

"He who learns but does not think, is lost! He who thinks but does not learn is in great danger."

"The essence of knowledge is, having it, to apply it; not having it, to confess your ignorance."

"It is not possible for one to teach others who cannot teach his own family."

"The superior man is modest in his speech but exceeds in his actions."

"He who merely knows right principles is not equal to him who loves them."

"To be able under all circumstances to practice five things constitutes perfect virtue; these five things are

gravity, generosity of soul, sincerity, earnestness and kindness."

"The object of the superior man is truth."

"A journey of a thousand miles begins with a single step."

"I hear and I forget. I see and I remember. I do and I understand."

"Only the wisest and stupidest of men never change."

"Our greatest glory is not in never falling, but in rising every time we fall."

"Real knowledge is to know the extent of one's ignorance."

"A man who does not plan long ahead will find trouble right at his door."

"Everything has its beauty but not everyone sees it."

"To know that one knows what one knows, and to know that one doesn't know what one doesn't know, there lies true wisdom."

"Without knowing the force of words, it is impossible to know men."

"Things that are done, it is needless to speak about...things that are past, it is needless to blame."

"The cautious seldom err."

"He who wishes to secure the good of others has already secured his own."

"To be wronged is nothing unless you continue to remember it."

"Learning without thought is labor lost thought without learning is perilous."

"It is only the wisest and the stupidest that cannot change."

"The expectations of life depend upon diligence the mechanic that would perfect his work must first sharpen his tools."

"Silence is a friend who will never betray."

"He does not preach what he practices till he has practiced what he preaches."

"He who learns but does not think, is lost He who thinks but does not learn is in great danger."

"If we don't know life, how can we know death"

"When you have faults, do not fear to abandon them."

"The perfecting of one's self is the fundamental base of all progress and all moral development."

"To see what is right, and not to do it, is want of courage or of principle."

"The essence of knowledge is, having it, to apply it not having it, to confess your ignorance."

"It does not matter how slowly you go so long as you do not stop."

"Ignorance is the night of the mind, but a night without moon and star."

"Wheresoever you go, go with all your heart."

"The wheel of fortune turns round incessantly, and who can say to himself, I shall to-day be uppermost."

"Heaven means to be one with God."

"The superior man acts before he speaks, and afterwards speaks according to his actions."

"We take greater pains to persuade others that we are happy than in endeavoring to think so ourselves."

"The superior man makes the difficulty to be overcome his first interest success only comes later."

"Looking at small advantages prevents great affairs from being accomplished."

"Better a diamond with a flaw than a pebble without."

"When you know a thing, to hold that you know it and when you do not know a thing, to allow that you do not know it - this is knowledge"

"By three methods we may learn wisdom: First, by reflection, which is noblest; Second, by imitation, which is easiest; and third by experience, which is the bitterest"

"Virtue is not left to stand alone. He who practices it will have neighbors."

"Wealth and rank are what people desire, but unless they be obtained in the right way they may not be possessed."

"What is the sound of one hand clapping"

"Fine words and an insinuating appearance are seldom associated with true virtue."

"Silence is the true friend that never betrays."

"I do not want a friend Who smiles when I smile Who weeps when I weep For my shadow in the pool Can do better than that."

"Do not use a cannon to kill a mosquito."

"Men's natures are alike, it is their habits that carry them far apart."

"Be not ashamed of mistakes and thus make them crimes."

"He who will not economize will have to agonize."

"Forget injuries, never forget kindnesses."

"Study the past if you would define the future."

"Respect yourself and others will respect you."

"They must often change who would be constant in happiness or wisdom."

"The superior man, when resting in safety, does not forget that danger may come. When in a state of security he does not forget the possibility of ruin. When all is orderly, he does not forget that disorder may come. Thus his person is not endangered, and his States and all their clans are preserved. "

"By nature, men are nearly alike by practice, they get to be wide apart."

"When anger rises, think of the consequences."

"What the superior man seeks is in himself what the small man seeks is in others."

"Have no friends not equal to yourself."

"When we see men of a contrary character, we should turn inwards and examine ourselves."

"He who speaks without modesty will find it difficult to make his words good."

"If a man withdraws his mind from the love of beauty, and applies it as sincerely to the love of the virtuous; if, in serving his parents, he can exert his utmost strength; if, in serving his prince, he can devote his life; if in his intercourse with his friends, his words are sincere - although men say that he has not learned, I will certainly say that he has. "

"He who exercises government by means of his virtue may be compared to the north polar star, which keeps its place and all the stars turn towards it. "
"He with whom neither slander that gradually soaks into the mind, nor statements that startle like a wound in the flesh, are successful may be called intelligent indeed."

"I have not seen a person who loved virtue, or one who hated what was not virtuous. He who loved virtue would esteem nothing above it."

"Is virtue a thing remote I wish to be virtuous, and lo Virtue is at hand."

"Hold faithfulness and sincerity as first principles."

"If a man takes no thought about what is distant, he will find sorrow near at hand."

"I am not one who was born in the possession of knowledge I am one who is fond of antiquity, and earnest in seeking it there."

"The superior man is modest in his speech, but exceeds in his actions."

"The man who in view of gain thinks of righteousness; who in the view of danger is prepared to give up his life; and who does not forget an old agreement however far back it extends - such a man may be reckoned a complete man."

"The man of virtue makes the difficulty to be overcome his first business, and success only a subsequent consideration."

"The determined scholar and the man of virtue will not seek to live at the expense of injuring their virtue. They will even sacrifice their lives to preserve their virtue complete."

"The scholar who cherishes the love of comfort is not fit to be deemed a scholar."

"The firm, the enduring, the simple, and the modest are near to virtue."

"Recompense injury with justice, and recompense kindness with kindness."

"The superior man cannot be known in little matters, but he may be entrusted with great concerns. The small man may not be entrusted with great concerns, but he may be known in little matters."

"The people may be made to follow a path of action, but they may not be made to understand it."

"To go beyond is as wrong as to fall short."

"What you do not want done to yourself, do not do to others."

"There are three things which the superior man guards against. In youth...lust. When he is strong...quarrelsomeness. When he is old...covetousness."

"Virtue is more to man than either water or fire. I have seen men die from treading on water and fire, but I have never seen a man die from treading the course of virtue."

"The superior man...does not set his mind either for anything, or against anything what is right he will follow."

"The superior man is satisfied and composed the mean man is always full of distress."

"Without an acquaintance with the rules of propriety, it is impossible for the character to be established."

"While you are not able to serve men, how can you serve spirits of the dead...While you do not know life, how can you know about death?"

"When we see men of worth, we should think of equaling them when we see men of a contrary character, we should turn inwards and examine ourselves"

"When a man's knowledge is sufficient to attain, and his virtue is not sufficient to enable him to hold, whatever he may have gained"

"With coarse rice to eat, with water to drink, and my bended arm for a pillow - I have still joy in the midst of these things."

Lao-Tsu

(600 and 300 B.C.E.)

Lao Tzu; (also Lao Tse, Lao Tu, Lao-Tzu, Lao-Tsu, Laotze, Laosi, Lao Zi, Laocius, and other variations) was a mystic philosopher of ancient China, and best known as the author of the Tao Te Ching. His association with the Tao Te Ching has led him to be traditionally considered the founder of Taoism (also spelled "Daoism"). He is also revered as a deity in most religious forms of the Taoist religion, which often refers to Laozi as Taishang Laojun, or "One of the Three Pure Ones". Laozi translated literally from Chinese means "old master" or "old one", and is generally considered honorific.

According to Chinese tradition, Laozi lived in the 6th century BC. Historians variously contend that Laozi is a synthesis of multiple historical figures, that he is a mythical figure, or that he actually lived in the 4th century BC, concurrent with the Hundred Schools of Thought and Warring States Period.

A central figure in Chinese culture, both nobility and common people claim Laozi in their lineage. Throughout history, Laozi's work has been embraced by various anti-authoritarian movements.

Excerpt from "TAO TEH KING" from the translation by by Dwight Goddard and Henri Borel:

I
WHAT IS THE TAO
The Tao that can be understood cannot be the primal, or cosmic, Tao, just as an idea that can be expressed in words cannot be the infinite idea.

And yet this ineffable Tao was the source of all spirit and matter, and being expressed was the mother of all created things.

Therefore not to desire the things of sense is to know the freedom of spirituality; and to desire is to learn the limitation of matter. These two things spirit and matter, so different in nature, have the same origin. This unity of origin is the mystery of mysteries, but it is the gateway to spirituality.

II
SELF-DEVELOPMENT
When every one recognizes beauty to be only a masquerade, then it is simply ugliness. In the same way goodness, if it is not sincere, is not goodness. So existence and non-existence are incompatible. The difficult and easy are mutually opposites. Just as the long and the short, p. 12 the high and the low, the loud and soft, the before and the behind, are all opposites and each reveals the other.

Therefore the wise man is not conspicuous in his affairs or given to much talking. Though troubles arise he is not irritated. He produces but does not own; he acts but claims no merit; he builds but does not dwell therein; and because he does not dwell therein he never departs.

III
QUIETING PEOPLE
Neglecting to praise the worthy deters people from emulating them; just as not prizing rare treasures deters a man from becoming a thief; or ignoring the things which awaken desire keeps the heart at rest.

Therefore the wise ruler does not suggest unnecessary things, but seeks to satisfy the minds of his people. He seeks to allay appetites but strengthen bones. He ever tries by keeping people in ignorance to keep them satisfied and those who have knowledge he restrains from evil. If he, himself, practices restraint then everything is in quietness.

IV
TAO, WITHOUT ORIGIN
The Tao appears to be emptiness but it is never exhausted. Oh, it is profound! It appears to have preceded everything. It dulls its own sharpness, unravels its own fetters, softens its own brightness, identifies itself with its own dust.

Oh, it is tranquil! It appears infinite; I do not know from what it proceeds. It even appears to be antecedent to the Lord.

V

IMPARTIALITY

Heaven and earth are not like humans, they are impartial. They regard all things as insignificant, as though they were playthings made of straw. The wise man is also impartial. To him all men are alike and unimportant. The space between heaven and earth is like a bellows, it is empty but does not collapse; it moves and more and more issues. A gossip is soon empty, it is doubtful if he can be impartial.

VI

THE INFINITUDE OF CREATIVE EFFORT

The Spirit of the perennial spring is said to be immortal, she is called the Mysterious One. The Mysterious One is typical of the source of heaven and earth. It is continually and endlessly issuing and without effort.

VII

HUMILITY

Heaven is eternal, earth is lasting. The reason why heaven and earth are eternal and lasting is because they do not live for themselves; that is the reason they will ever endure.

Therefore the wise man will keep his personality out of sight and because of so doing he will become notable. He subordinates his personality and therefore it is preserved.

Is it not because he is disinterested, that his own interests are conserved?

VIII

THE NATURE OF GOODNESS

True goodness is like water, in that it benefits everything and harms nothing. Like water it ever seeks the lowest place, the place that all others avoid. It is closely kin to the Tao.

For a dwelling it chooses the quiet meadow; for a heart the circling eddy. In generosity it is kind; in speech it is sincere; in authority it is order; in affairs it is ability; in movement it is rhythm.

Inasmuch as it is always peaceable it is never rebuked.

IX
MODERATION

Continuing to fill a pail after it is full the water will be wasted. Continuing to grind an axe after it is sharp will soon wear it away.

Who can protect a public hall crowded with gold and jewels? The pride of wealth and position brings about their own misfortune. To win true merit, to preserve just fame, the personality must be retiring. This is the heavenly Tao.

X
WHAT IS POSSIBLE

By patience the animal spirits can be disciplined. By self-control one can unify the character. By close attention to the will, compelling gentleness, one can become like a little child. By purifying the subconscious desires one may be without fault. In ruling his country, if the wise magistrate loves his people, he can avoid compulsion.

In measuring out rewards, the wise magistrate will act like a mother bird. While sharply penetrating into every corner, he may appear to be unsuspecting. While quickening and feeding his people, he will be producing but without pride of ownership. He will benefit but without claim of reward. He will persuade, but not compel by force. This is teh, the profoundest virtue.

XI
THE VALUE OF NON-EXISTENCE

Although the wheel has thirty spokes its utility lies in the emptiness of the hub. The jar is made by kneading clay, but its usefulness consists in its capacity. A room is made by cutting out windows and doors through the walls, but the space the walls contain measures the room's value.

In the same way matter is necessary to form, but the value of reality lies in its immateriality.

(Or thus: a material body is necessary to existence, but the value of a life is measured by its immaterial soul.)

XII
AVOIDING DESIRE
An excess of light blinds the human eye; an excess of noise ruins the ear; an excess of condiments deadens the taste. The effect of too much horse racing and hunting is bad, and the lure of hidden treasure tempts one to do evil.

Therefore the wise man attends to the inner significance of things and does not concern himself with outward appearances. Therefore he ignores matter and seeks the spirit.

XIII
LOATHING SHAME
Favor and disgrace are alike to be feared, just as too great care or anxiety are bad for the body.

Why are favor and disgrace alike to be feared? To be favored is humiliating; to obtain it is as much to be dreaded as to lose it. To lose favor is to be in disgrace and of course is to be dreaded.

Why are excessive care and great anxiety alike bad for one? The very reason I have anxiety is because I have a body. If I have not body why would I be anxious?

Therefore if he who administers the empire, esteems it as his own body, then he is worthy to be trusted with the empire.

XIV
IN PRAISE OF THE PROFOUND
It is unseen because it is colorless; it is unheard because it is soundless; when seeking to grasp it, it eludes one, because it is incorporeal.

Because of these qualities it cannot be examined, and yet they form an essential unity. Superficially it appears abstruse, but in its depths it is not obscure. It has been nameless forever! It appears and then disappears. It is what is known as the form of the formless, the image of the imageless. It is called the transcendental, its face (or destiny) cannot be seen in front, or its back (or origin) behind.

But by holding fast to the Tao of the ancients, the wise man may understand the present, because he knows the origin of the past. This is the clue to the Tao.

XV
THAT WHICH REVEALS TEH
In olden times the ones who were considered worthy to be called masters were subtle, spiritual, profound, wise. Their thoughts could not be easily understood.

Since they were hard to understand I will try to make them clear. They were cautious like men wading a river in winter. They were reluctant like men who feared their neighbors. They were reserved like guests in the presence of their host. They were elusive like ice at the point of melting. They were like unseasoned wood. They were like a valley between high mountains. They were obscure like troubled waters. (They were cautious because they were conscious of the deeper meanings of life and its possibilities.)

We can clarify troubled waters by slowly quieting them. We can bring the unconscious to life by slowly moving them. But he who has the secret of the Tao does not desire for more. Being content, he is able to mature without desire to be newly fashioned.

XVI
RETURNING TO THE SOURCE
Seek to attain an open mind (the summit of vacuity). Seek composure (the essence of tranquility).

All things are in process, rising and returning. Plants come to blossom, but only to return to the root. Returning to the root is like seeking tranquility; it is moving towards its destiny. To move toward destiny is like eternity. To know eternity is enlightenment, and not to recognize eternity brings disorder and evil.

Knowing eternity makes one comprehensive; comprehension makes one broadminded; breadth of vision brings nobility; nobility is like heaven.

The heavenly is like Tao. Tao is the Eternal. The decay of the body is not to be feared.

XVII
SIMPLICITY OF HABIT

When great men rule, subjects know little of their existence. Rulers who are less great win the affection and praise of their subjects. A common ruler is feared by his subjects, and an unworthy ruler is despised.

When a ruler lacks faith, you may seek in vain for it among his subjects.

How carefully a wise ruler chooses his words. He performs deeds, and accumulates merit! Under such a ruler the people think they are ruling themselves.

XVIII
THE PALLIATION OF THE INFERIOR

When the great Tao is lost sight of, we still have the idea of benevolence and righteousness. Prudence and wisdom come to mind when we see great hypocrisy. When relatives are! unfriendly, we still have the teachings of filial piety and paternal affection. When the state and the clan are in confusion and disorder, we still have the ideals of loyalty and faithfulness.

XIX
RETURN TO SIMPLICITY

Abandon the show of saintliness and relinquish excessive prudence, then people will benefit a hundredfold. Abandon ostentatious benevolence and conspicuous righteousness, then people will return p. 20 to the primal virtues of filial piety and parental affection. Abandon cleverness and relinquish gains, then thieves and robbers will disappear.

Here are three fundamentals on which to depend, wherein culture is insufficient. Therefore let all men hold to that which is reliable, namely, recognize simplicity, cherish purity, reduce one's possessions, diminish one's desires.

XX
THE OPPOSITE OF THE COMMONPLACE

Avoid learning if you would have no anxiety. The "yes" and the "yea" differ very little, but the contrast between good and evil is very great. That which is not feared by the people is not worth fearing. But, oh, the difference, the desolation, the vastness, between ignorance and the limitless expression of the Tao.

XXI
THE HEART OF EMPTINESS

All the innumerable forms of teh correspond to the norm of Tao, but the nature of the Tao's activity is infinitely abstract and illusive. Illusive and obscure, indeed, but at its heart are forms and types. Vague and illusive, indeed, but at its heart is all being. Unfathomable and obscure, indeed, but at its heart is all spirit, and spirit is reality. At its heart is truth.

From of old its expression is unceasing, it has been present at all beginnings. How do I know that its nature is thus? By this same Tao.

XXII
INCREASE BY HUMILITY

At that time the deficient will be made perfect; the distorted will be straightened; the empty will be filled; the worn out will be renewed; those having little will obtain and those having much will be overcome.

Therefore the wise man, embracing unity as he does, will become the world's model. Not pushing himself forward he will become enlightened; not asserting himself he will become distinguished; not boasting of himself he will acquire merit; not approving himself he will endure. Forasmuch as he will not quarrel, the world will not quarrel with him.

Is the old saying, "The crooked shall be made straight," a false saying? Indeed, no! They will be perfected and return rejoicing.

XXIII
EMPTINESS AND NOT-DOING (WU WEI)
Taciturnity is natural to man. A whirlwind never outlasts the morning, nor a violent rain the day. What is the cause? It is heaven and p. 22 earth. If even heaven and earth are not constant, much less can man be.

Therefore he who pursues his affairs in the spirit of Tao will become Tao-like. He who pursues his affairs with teh, will become teh-like. He who pursues his affairs with loss, identifies himself with loss.

He who identifies himself with Tao, Tao rejoices to guide. He who identifies himself with teh, teh rejoices to reward. And he who identifies himself with loss, loss rejoices to ruin.

If his faith fail, he will receive no reward of faith.

XXIV
TROUBLES AND MERIT
It is not natural to stand on tiptoe, or being astride one does not walk. One who displays himself is not bright, or one who asserts himself cannot shine. A self-approving man has no merit, nor does one who praises himself grow.

The relation of these things (self-display, self-assertion, self-approval) to Tao is the same as offal is to food. They are excrescences from the system; they are detestable; Tao does not dwell in them.

XXV
DESCRIBING THE MYSTERIOUS
There is Being that is all-inclusive and that existed before Heaven and Earth. Calm, indeed, and incorporeal! It is alone and changeless!

Everywhere it functions unhindered. It thereby becomes the world's mother. I do not know its nature; if I try to characterize it, I will call it Tao.

If forced to give it a name, I will call it the Great. The Great is evasive, the evasive is the distant, the distant is ever coming near. Tao is Great. So is Heaven great, and so is Earth and so also is the representative of Heaven and Earth.

Man is derived from nature, nature is derived from Heaven, Heaven is derived from Tao. Tao is self-derived.

XXVI
THE VIRTUE (TEH) OF DIGNITY
The heavy is the root of the light; the quiet is master of motion. Therefore the wise man in all the experience of the day will not depart from dignity. Though he be surrounded with sights that are magnificent, he will remain calm and unconcerned.

How does it come to pass that the Emperor, master of ten thousand chariots, has lost the mastery of the Empire? Because being flippant himself, he has lost the respect of his subjects; being passionate himself, he has lost the control of the Empire.

XXVII
THE FUNCTION OF SKILL
Good walkers leave no tracks, good speakers make no errors, good counters need no abacus, good wardens have no need for bolts and locks for no one can get by them. Good binders can dispense with rope and cord, yet none can unloose their hold.

Therefore the wise man trusting in goodness always saves men, for there is no outcast to him. Trusting in goodness he saves all things for there is nothing valueless to him. This is recognizing concealed values.

Therefore the good man is the instructor of the evil man, and the evil man is the good man's wealth. He who does not esteem his instructors or value his wealth, though he be otherwise intelligent, becomes confused. Herein lies the significance of spirituality.

XXVIII
RETURNING TO SIMPLICITY
He who knows his manhood and understands his womanhood becomes useful like the valleys of earth (which bring water). Being like the valleys of earth, eternal vitality (teh) will not depart from him, he will come again to the nature of a little child.

He who knows his innocence and recognizes his sin becomes the world's model. Being a world's model, infinite teh will not fail, he will return to the Absolute.

He who knows the glory of his nature and recognizes also his limitations becomes useful like the world's valleys. Being like the world's valleys, eternal teh will not fail him, he will revert to simplicity.

Radiating simplicity he will make of men vessels of usefulness. The wise man then will employ them as officials and chiefs. A great administration of such will harm no one.

XXIX
NOT FORCING THINGS (WU WEI)
One who desires to take and remake the Empire will fail. The Empire is a divine thing that cannot be remade. He who attempts it will only mar it.

He who seeks to grasp it, will lose it. People differ, some lead, others follow; some are ardent, others are formal; some are strong, others weak; some succeed, others fail. Therefore the wise man practices moderation; he abandons pleasure, extravagance and indulgence.

XXX
BE STINGY OF WAR
When the magistrate follows Tao, he has no need to resort to force of arms to strengthen the Empire, because his business methods alone will show good returns.

Briars and thorns grow rank where an army camps. Bad harvests are the sequence of a great war. The good ruler will be resolute and then stop, he dare not take by force. One should be resolute but not boastful; resolute but not haughty; resolute but not arrogant; resolute but yielding when it cannot be avoided; resolute but he must not resort to violence.

By a resort to force, things flourish for a time but then decay. This is not like the Tao and that which is not Tao-like will soon cease.

XXXI
AVOIDING WAR

Even successful arms, among all implements, are unblessed. All men come to detest them. Therefore the one who follows Tao does not rely on them. Arms are of all tools unblessed, they are not the implements of a wise man. Only as a last resort does he use them.

Peace and quietude are esteemed by the wise man, and even when victorious he does not rejoice, because rejoicing over a victory is the same as rejoicing over the killing of men. If he rejoices over killing men, do you think he will ever really master the Empire?

In propitious affairs the place of honor is the left, but in unpropitious affairs we honor the right.

The strong man while at home esteems the left as the place of honor, but when armed for war it is as though he esteems the right hand, the place of less honor.

Thus a funeral ceremony is so arranged. The place of a subordinate army officer is also on the left and the place of his superior officer is on the right. The killing of men fills multitudes with sorrow; we lament with tears because of it, and rightly honor the victor as if he was attending a funeral ceremony.

XXXII
THE VIRTUE (TEH) OF HOLINESS

Tao in its eternal aspect is unnamable. Its simplicity appears insignificant, but the whole world cannot control it. If princes and kings employ it every one of themselves will pay willing homage. Heaven and Earth by it are harmoniously combined and drop sweet dew. People will have no need of rulers, because of themselves they will be righteous.

As soon as Tao expresses itself in orderly creation then it becomes comprehensible. When one recognizes the presence of Tao he understands where to stop. Knowing where to stop he is free from danger.

To illustrate the nature of Tao's place in the universe: Tao is like the brooks and streams in their relation to the great rivers and the ocean.

XXXIII
THE VIRTUE (TEH) OF DISCRIMINATION

He who knows others is intelligent; he who understands himself is enlightened; he who is able to conquer others has force, but he who is able to control himself is mighty. He who appreciates contentment is wealthy.

He who dares to act has nerve; if he can maintain his position he will endure, but he, who dying does not perish, is immortal.

XXXIV
THE PERFECTION OF TRUST

Great Tao is all pervading! It can be on both the right hand and the left. Everything relies upon it for their existence, and it does not fail them. It acquires merit but covets not the title. It lovingly nourishes everything, but does not claim the rights of ownership. It has no desires, it can be classed with the small. Everything returns to it, yet it does not claim the right of ownership. It can be classed with the great.

Therefore the wise man to the end will not pose as a great man, and by so doing will express his true greatness.

XXXV
THE VIRTUE (TEH) OF BENEVOLENCE

The world will go to him who grasps this Great Principle; they will seek and not be injured, they will find contentment, peace and rest.

Music and dainties attract the passing people, while Tao's reality seen- is insipid. Indeed it has no taste, when looked at there is not enough seen to be prized, when listened for, it can scarcely be heard, but, the use of it is inexhaustible.

XXXVI
EXPLANATION OF A PARADOX

That which has a tendency to contract must first have been extended; that which has a tendency to weaken itself must first have been strong; that which shows a tendency to destroy itself must first have been raised up; that which shows a tendency to scatter must first have been gathered.

This is the explanation of a seeming contradiction: the tender and yielding conquer the rigid and strong (i.e., spirit is stronger than matter, persuasion than force). The fish would be foolish to seek escape from its natural environment. There is no gain to a nation to compel by a show of force.

XXXVII
ADMINISTERING THE GOVERNMENT

Tao is apparently inactive (wu wei) and yet nothing remains undone. If princes and kings desire to keep) everything in order, they must first reform themselves. (If princes and kings would follow the example of Tao, then all things will reform themselves.) If they still desire to change, I would pacify them by the simplicity of the ineffable Tao.

This simplicity will end desire, and if desire be absent there is quietness. All people will of themselves be satisfied.

XXXVIII
A DISCUSSION ABOUT TEH

Essential teh makes no show of virtue, and therefore it is really virtuous. Inferior virtue never loses sight of itself and therefore it is no longer virtue. Essential virtue is characterized by lack of self-assertion (wu wei) and therefore is unpretentious. Inferior virtue is acting a part and thereby is only pretense.

Superior benevolence in a way is acting but does not thereby become pretentious. Excessive righteousness is acting and does thereby become pretentious. Excessive propriety is acting, but where no one responds to it, it stretches its arm and enforces obedience.

Therefore when one loses Tao there is still teh; one may lose teh and benevolence remains; one may forsake benevolence and still hold to righteousness; one may lose righteousness and propriety remains.

Propriety, alone, reduces loyalty and good faith to a shadow, and it is the beginning of disorder. Tradition is the mere flower of the Tao and had its origin in ignorance.

Therefore the great man of affairs conforms to the spirit and not to external appearance. He goes on to fruitage and does not rest in the show of blossom. He avoids mere propriety and practices true benevolence.

XXXIX
THE ROOT OF AUTHORITY

It has been said of old, only those who attain unity attain self-hood. . . . Heaven attained unity and thereby is space. Earth attained unity, thereby it is solid. Spirit attained unity, thereby it became mind. Valleys attained unity, therefore rivers flow down them. All things have unity and thereby have life. Princes and kings as they attain unity become standards of conduct for the nation. And the highest unity is that which produces unity.

If heaven were not space it might crack, if earth were not solid it might bend. If spirits were not unified into mind they might vanish, if valleys were not adapted to rivers they would be parched. Everything if it were not for life would burn up. Even princes and kings if they overestimate themselves and cease to be standards will presumably fall.

Therefore nobles find their roots among the commoners; the high is always founded upon the low. The reason why princes and kings speak of themselves as orphans, inferiors and unworthy, is because they recognize that their roots run down to the common life; is it not so?

If a carriage goes to pieces it is no longer a carriage, its unity is gone. A true self-hood does not desire to be overvalued as a gem, nor to be undervalued as a mere stone.

XL
AVOIDING ACTIVITY

Retirement is characteristic of Tao just as weakness appears to be a characteristic of its activity.

Heaven and earth and everything are produced from existence, but existence comes from nonexistence. . . .

XLI
THE UNREALITY OF APPEARANCE
The superior scholar when he considers Tao earnestly practices it; an average scholar listening to Tao sometimes follows it and sometimes loses it; an inferior scholar listening to Tao ridicules it. Were it not thus ridiculed it could not be regarded as Tao.

Therefore the writer says: Those who are most illumined by Tao are the most obscure. Those advanced in Tao are most retiring. Those best guided by Tao are the least prepossessing.

The high in virtue (teh) resemble a lowly valley; the whitest are most likely to be put to shame; the broadest in virtue resemble the inefficient. The most firmly established in virtue resemble the remiss. The simplest chastity resembles the fickle, the greatest square has no corner, the largest vessel is never filled. The greatest sound is void of speech, the greatest form has no shape. Tao is obscure and without p. 33 name, and yet it is precisely this Tao that alone can give and complete.

XLII
THE TRANSFORMATION OF TAO
Tao produces unity; unity produces duality; duality produces trinity; trinity produces all things. All things bear the negative principle (yin) and embrace the positive principle (yang). Immaterial vitality, the third principle (chi), makes them harmonious.

Those things which are detested by the common people, namely to be called orphans, inferiors, and unworthies, are the very things kings and lords take for titles. There are some things which it is a gain to lose, and a loss to gain.

I am teaching the same things which are taught by others. But the strong and aggressive: ones do not obtain a natural death (i.e., self-confident teachers do not succeed). I alone expound the basis of the doctrine of the Tao.

XLIII
THE FUNCTION OF THE UNIVERSAL
The most tender things of creation race over the hardest.

A non-material existence enters into the most impenetrable.

I therefore recognize an advantage in the doctrine of not doing (wu wei) and not speaking

XLIV
PRECEPTS
Which is nearer, a name or a person? Which is more, personality or treasure? Is it more painful to gain or to suffer loss?

Extreme indulgence certainly greatly wastes. Much hoarding certainly invites severe loss.

A contented person is not despised. One who knows when to stop is not endangered; he will be able therefore to continue.

XLV
THE VIRTUE (TEH) OF GREATNESS
Extreme perfection seems imperfect, its function is not exhausted. Extreme fullness appears empty, its function is not exercised.

Extreme straightness appears crooked; great skill, clumsy; great eloquence, stammering. Motion conquers cold, quietude conquers heat. Not greatness but purity and clearness are the world's standard.

XLVI
LIMITATION OF DESIRE
When the world yields to Tao, race horses will be used to haul manure. When the world ignores Tao war horses are pastured on the public common.

There is no sin greater than desire. There is no misfortune greater than discontent. There is no calamity greater than acquisitiveness.

Therefore to know extreme contentment is simply to be content.

XLVII
SEEING THE DISTANT
Not going out of the door I have knowledge of the world. Not peeping through the window I perceive heaven's Tao. The more one wanders to a distance the less he knows.

Therefore the wise man does not wander about but he understands, he does not see things but he defines them, he does not labor yet he completes.

XLVIII
TO FORGET KNOWLEDGE
He who attends daily to learning increases in learning. He who practices Tao daily diminishes. Again and again he humbles himself. Thus he attains to non-doing (wu wei). He practices non-doing and yet there is nothing left undone.

To command the empire one must not employ craft. If one uses craft he is not fit to command the empire.

XLIX
THE VIRTUE (TEH) OF TRUST
The wise man has no fixed heart; in the hearts of the people he finds his own. The good he treats p. 36 with goodness; the not-good he also treats with goodness, for teh is goodness. The faithful ones he treats with good faith; the unfaithful he also treats with good faith, for teh is good faith.

The wise man lives in the world but he lives cautiously, dealing with the world cautiously. He universalizes his heart; the people give him their eyes and ears, but he treats them as his children.

L
ESTEEM LIFE
Life is a going forth; death is a returning home. Of ten, three are seeking life, three are seeking death, and three are dying. What is the reason? Because they live in life's experience. (Only one is immortal.)

I hear it said that the sage when he travels is never attacked by rhinoceros or tiger, and when coming among soldiers does not fear their weapons. The rhinoceros would find no place to horn him, nor the tiger a place for his claws, nor could soldiers wound him. What is the reason? Because he is invulnerable.

LI
TEH AS A NURSE
Tao gives life to all creatures; teh feeds them; materiality shapes them; energy completes them. p. 37 Therefore among all things there is none that does not honor Tao and esteem teh. Honor for Tao and esteem for teh is never compelled, it is always spontaneous. Therefore Tao gives life to them, but teh nurses them, raises them, nurtures, completes, matures, rears, protects them.

Tao gives life to them but makes no claim of ownership; teh forms them but makes no claim upon them, raises them but does not rule them. This is profound vitality (teh).

RETURN TO ORIGIN
When creation began, Tao became the world's mother. When one knows one's mother he will m turn know that he is her son. When he recognizes his sonship, he will in turn keep to his mother and to the end of life will be free from danger.

He who closes his mouth and shuts his sense gates will be free from trouble to the end of life. He who opens his mouth and meddles with affairs cannot be free from trouble even to the end of life.

To recognize one's insignificance is called enlightenment. To keep one's sympathy is called strength. He who uses Tao's light returns to Tao's enlightenment and does not surrender his person to perdition. This is called practicing the eternal.

LIII
GAIN BY INSIGHT
Even if one has but a little knowledge he can walk in the ways of the great Tao; it is only self-assertion that one need fear.

The great Tao (Way) is very plain, but people prefer the bypaths.

When the palace is very splendid, the fields are likely to be very weedy, and the granaries empty. To wear ornaments and gay colors, to carry sharp swords, to be excessive in eating and drinking, and to have wealth and treasure in abundance is to know the pride of robbers. This is contrary to Tao.

LIV
TO CULTIVATE INTUITION
The thing that is well planted is not easily uprooted. The thing that is well guarded is not easily taken away. If one has sons and grandsons, the offering of ancestral worship will not soon cease.

He who practices Tao in his person shows that his teh is real. The family that practices it shows that their teh is abounding. The township that practices it shows that their teh is enduring. The state that practices it shows that their teh is prolific. The empire that practices it reveals that teh is universal. Thereby one person becomes a test of other persons, one family of other families, one town of other towns, one county of other counties, and one empire of all empires.

How do I know that this test is universal? By this same Tao.

LV
TO VERIFY THE MYSTERIOUS
The essence of teh is comparable to the state of a young boy. Poisonous insects will not sting him, wild beasts will not seize him, birds of prey will not attack him. The bones are weak, the muscles are tender, it is true, but his grasp is firm.

He does not yet know the relation of the sexes, but he has perfect organs, nevertheless. His spirit is virile, indeed! He can sob and cry all day without becoming hoarse, his harmony (as a child) is perfect indeed!

To recognize this harmony (for growth) is to know the eternal'. To recognize the eternal is to know enlightenment. To increase life (to cause things to grow) is to know blessedness. To be conscious of an inner fecundity is strength. Things fully grown are about to decay, they are the opposite of Tao. The opposite of Tao soon ceases.

LVI
THE TEH OF THE MYSTERIOUS
The one who knows does not speak; the one who speaks does not know. The wise man shuts his mouth and closes his gates. He softens his sharpness, unravels his tangles, dims his brilliancy, and reckons himself with the mysterious.

He is inaccessible to favor or hate; he cannot be reached by profit or injury; he cannot be honored or humiliated. Thereby he is honored by all.

LVII
THE HABIT OF SIMPLICITY
The empire is administered with righteousness; the army is directed by craft; the people are captivated by non-diplomacy. How do I know it is so? By this same Tao.

Among people the more restrictions and prohibitions there are, the poorer they become. The more people have weapons, the more the state is in confusion. The more people are artful and cunning the more abnormal things occur. The more laws and orders are issued the more thieves and robbers abound.

Therefore the wise man says: If a ruler practices wu wei the people will reform of themselves. If I love quietude the people will of themselves become righteous. If I avoid profit-making the people will of themselves become prosperous. If I limit my desires the people will of themselves become simple.

LVIII
ADAPTATION TO CHANGE
When an administration is unostentatious the people are simple. When an administration is inquisitive, the people are needy. Misery, alas, supports happiness. Happiness, alas, conceals misery. Who knows its limits? It never ceases. The normal becomes the abnormal. The good in turn becomes unlucky. The people's confusion is felt daily for a long time.

Therefore the wise man is square, yet does not injure, he is angular but does not annoy. He is upright but is not cross. He is bright but not glaring.

LIX
TO KEEP TAO
In governing the people and in worshipping heaven nothing surpasses moderation. To value moderation, one must form the habit early. Its early acquisition will result in storing and accumulating vitality. By storing and accumulating vitality nothing is impossible.

If nothing is impossible then one is ignorant of his limits. If one does not know his limitations, one may possess the state. He who possesses moderation is thereby lasting and enduring. It is like having deep roots and a strong stem. This is of long life and enduring insight the Tao (way).

LX
TO MAINTAIN POSITION
One should govern a great state as one fries small fish (i.e., do not scale or clean them).

With Tao one may successfully rule the Empire. Ghosts will not frighten, gods will not harm, neither will wise men mislead the people. Since nothing frightens or harms the people, teh will abide.

LXI
THE TEH OF HUMILITY
A great state that is useful is like a bond of unity within the Empire; it is the Empire's wife.

The female controls the male by her quietude and submission. Thus a great state by its service to smaller states wins their allegiance. A small state by submission to a great state wins an influence over them. Thus some stoop to conquer, and others stoop and conquer.

Great states can have no higher purpose than to federate states and feed the people. Small states can have no higher purpose than to enter a federation and serve the people. Both alike, each in his own way, gain their end, but to do so, the greater must practice humility.

LXII
THE PRACTICE OF TAO
The Tao is the asylum of all things; the good man's treasure, the bad man's last resort. With beautiful words one may sell goods but in winning people one can accomplish more by kindness. Why should a man be thrown away for his evil? To conserve him was the Emperor appointed and the three ministers.

Better than being in the presence of the Emperor and riding with four horses, is sitting and explaining this Tao.

The reason the Ancients esteemed Tao was because if sought it was obtained, and because by it he that hath sin could be saved. Is it not so? Therefore the world honors Tao.

LXIII
A CONSIDERATION OF BEGINNINGS
One should avoid assertion (wu wei) and practice inaction. One should learn to find taste in the tasteless, to enlarge the small things, and multiply the few. He should respond to hatred with kindness. He should resolve a difficulty while it is easy, and manage a great thing while it is small. Surely all the world's difficulties arose from slight causes, and all the world's great affairs had small beginnings.

Therefore the wise man avoids to the end participation in great affairs and by so doing establishes his greatness.

Rash promises are lacking in faith and many things that appear easy are full of difficulties. Therefore the wise man considers every thing difficult and so to the end he has no difficulties.

LXIV
CONSIDER THE INSIGNIFICANT
That which is at rest is easily restrained, that which has not yet appeared is easily prevented. The weak is easily broken, the scanty is easily scattered. Consider a difficulty before it arises, and administer

affairs before they become disorganized. A tree that it takes both arms to encircle grew from a tiny rootlet.

A pagoda of nine stories was erected by placing small bricks. A journey of three thousand miles begins with one step. If one tries to improve a thing, he mars it; if he seizes it, he loses it. The wise man, therefore, not attempting to form things does not mar them, and not grasping after things he does not lose them. The people in their rush for business are ever approaching success but continually failing. One must be as careful to the end as at the beginning if he is to succeed.

Therefore the wise man desires to be free from desire, he does not value the things that are difficult of attainment. He learns to be unlearned, he returns to that which all others ignore. In that spirit he helps all things toward their natural development, but dares not interfere.

LXV
THE TEH OF SIMPLICITY
In the olden days those who obeyed the spirit of Tao did not enlighten the people but kept them simple hearted.

The reason people are difficult to govern is because of their smartness; likewise to govern a people with guile is a curse; and to govern them with simplicity is a blessing. He who p. 45 remembers these two things is a model ruler. Always to follow this standard and rule is teh, the profound.

Profound teh is deep indeed and far reaching. The very opposite of common things, but by it one obtains obedient subjects.

LXVI
TO SUBORDINATE SELF
The reason rivers and seas are called the kings of the valley is because they keep below them.

Therefore the wise man desiring to be above his people must in his demeanor keep below them; wishing to benefit his people, he must ever keep himself out of sight.

The wise man dwells above, yet the people do not feel the burden; he is the leader and the people suffer no harm. Therefore the world rejoices to exalt him and never wearies of him.

Because he will not quarrel with anyone, no one can quarrel with him.

LXVII
THREE TREASURES

All the world calls Tao great, yet it is by nature immaterial. It is because a thing is seemingly unreal that it is great. If a man affects to be great, how long can he conceal his mediocrity?

Tao has three treasures which he guards and cherishes. The first is called compassion; the second is called economy; the third is called humility. A man that is compassionate can 'be truly brave; if a man is economical he can be generous; if he is humble he can become a useful servant.

If one discards compassion and is still brave, abandons economy and is still generous, forsakes humility and still seeks to be serviceable, his days are numbered. On the contrary if one is truly compassionate, in battle he will be a conqueror and in defence he will be secure. When even Heaven helps people it is because of compassion that she does so.

LXVIII
COMPLIANCE WITH HEAVEN

He who excels as a soldier is the one who is not warlike; he who fights the best fight is not wrathful; he who best conquers an enemy is not quarrelsome; he who best employs people is obedient himself.

This is the virtue of not-quarreling, this is the secret of bringing out other men's ability, this is complying with Heaven. Since of old it is considered the greatest virtue (teh).

LXIX
THE FUNCTION OF THE MYSTERIOUS

A military expert has said: I do not dare put myself forward as a host, but always act as a guest. I hesitate to advance an inch, but am willing to withdraw a foot.

This is advancing by not advancing, it is winning without arms, it is charging without hostility, it is seizing without weapons. There is no mistake greater than making light of an enemy. By making light of an enemy we lose our treasure.

Therefore when well-matched armies come to conflict, the one who is conscious of his weakness conquers.

LXX
THE DIFFICULTY OF UNDERSTANDING
My words are very easy to understand and very easy to put into practice, yet in all the world no one appears to understand them or to practice them.

Words have an ancestor (a preceding idea), deeds have a master (a preceding purpose), and just as these are often not understood, so I am not understood.

They who understand me are very few, and on that account I am worthy of honor. The wise man wears wool (rather than silk) and keeps his gems out of sight.

LXXI
THE DISEASE OF KNOWLEDGE
To recognize one's ignorance of unknowable things is mental health, and to be ignorant of knowable things is sickness. Only by grieving over ignorance of knowable things are we in mental health. The wise man is wise because he understands his ignorance and is grieved over it.

LXXII
TO CHERISH ONE'S SELF
When people are too ignorant to fear the fearsome thing, then it will surely come. Do not make the place where they dwell confining, the life they live wearisome. If they are let alone, they will not become restless. Therefore the wise man while not understanding himself regards himself, while cherishing he does not overvalue himself. Therefore he discards flattery and prefers regard.

LXXIII
ACTION IS DANGEROUS
Courage carried to daring leads to death. Courage restrained by caution leads to life. These two things, courage and caution, are sometimes beneficial and sometimes harmful. Some things are rejected by heaven, who can tell the reason? Therefore the wise man deems all acting difficult.

The Tao of heaven does not quarrel, yet it conquers. It speaks not, yet its response is good. It issues no summons but things come to it naturally because its devices are good. Heaven's net is vast, indeed! its meshes are wide but it loses nothing.

LXXIV
OVERCOMING DELUSIONS
If the people do not fear death, how can one frighten them with death? If we teach people to fear death, then when one rebels he can be seized and executed; after that who will dare to rebel?

There is always an officer to execute a murderer, but if one takes the place of the executioner, it is like taking the place of a skilled carpenter at his hewing. If one takes the place of the skilled carpenter he is liable to cut himself. (Therefore do not interfere with Tao.)

LXXV
LOSS BY GREEDINESS
Starvation of a people comes when an official appropriates to himself too much of the taxes. The reason a people are difficult to govern is because the officials are too meddlesome; the people make light of death because they are so absorbed in life's interests. The one who is not absorbed in life is more moral than he who esteems life.

LXXVI
BEWARE OF STRENGTH
When a man is living he is tender and fragile. When he dies he is hard and stiff. It is the same with everything, the grass and trees, in life, are tender and delicate, but when they die they become rigid and dry.

Therefore those who are hard and stiff belong to death's domain, while the tender and weak belong to the realm of life.

Therefore soldiers are most invincible when they will not conquer. When a tree is grown to its greatest strength it is doomed. The strong and the great stay below; the tender and weak rise above.

LXXVII
TAO OF HEAVEN

Tao of heaven resembles the stretching of a bow. The mighty it humbles, the lowly it exalts. They who have abundance it diminishes and gives to them who have need.

That is Tao of heaven; it depletes those who abound, and completes those who lack.

The human way is not so. Men take from those who lack to give to those who already abound. Where is the man who by his abundance can best serve the world?

The wise man makes but claims not, he accomplishes merit, yet is not attached to it, neither does he display his excellence. Is it not so?

LXXVIII
TRUST AND FAITH

In the world nothing is more fragile than water, and yet of all the agencies that attack hard substances nothing can surpass it.

Of all things there is nothing that can take the place of Tao. By it the weak are conquerors of the strong, the pliable are conquerors of the rigid. In the world every one knows this, but none practice it.

Therefore the wise man declares: he who is guilty of the country's sin may be the priest at the altar. He who is to blame for the country's misfortunes, is often the Empire's Sovereign. True words are often paradoxical.

LXXIX
ENFORCING CONTRACTS

When reconciling great hatred there will some remain. How can it be made good?

Therefore the wise man accepts the debit side of the account and does not have to enforce payment from others. They who have virtue (teh) keep their obligations, they who have no virtue insist on their rights. Tao of heaven has no favorites but always helps the good man.

LXXX
CONTENTMENT
In a small country with few people let there be officers over tens and hundreds but not to exercise power. Let the people be not afraid of death, nor desire to move to a distance. Then though there be ships and carriages, they will have no occasion to use them. Though there be armor and weapons there will be no occasion for donning them. The people can return to knotted cords for their records, they can delight in their food, be proud of their clothes, be content with their dwellings, rejoice in their customs.

Other states may be close neighbors, their cocks and dogs may be mutually heard, people will come to old age and die but will have no desire to go or come.

LXXXI
THE NATURE OF THE ESSENTIAL
Faithful words are often not pleasant; pleasant words are often not faithful. Good men do not dispute; the ones who dispute are not good. The learned men are often not the wise men, nor the wise men, the learned. The wise man does not hoard, but ever working for others, he will the more exceedingly acquire. Having given to others freely, he himself will have in plenty. Tao of heaven benefits but does not injure. The wise man's Tao leads him to act but not to quarrel.

VALEDICTORY
PART OF THE 20TH SONNET
Common people are joyful; they celebrate a feast day; they flock to a pavilion in spring time. I alone am calm, as one who has as yet received no omen; I am as a babe who has not learned to smile. I am forlorn, like a homeless wanderer! Common people have plenty; I alone am in want. I am a foolish man at heart! I am ignorant.

Common people are vivacious and smart, I alone am dull and confused.

Knowledge of the Tao, how vast! I am like a sailor far beyond a place of anchorage, adrift on a boundless ocean. Common people are useful, I am awkward. I stand in contrast to them--but oh, the prize I seek is food from our Mother Tao!

Socrates

(469–399 B.C.E.)

Socrates was a classical Greek Athenian philosopher. Credited as one of the founders of Western philosophy, he is an enigmatic figure known chiefly through the accounts of later classical writers, especially the writings of his students Plato and Xenophon, and the plays of his contemporary Aristophanes. Many would claim that Plato's dialogues are the most comprehensive accounts of Socrates to survive from antiquity.

Through his portrayal in Plato's dialogues, Socrates has become renowned for his contribution to the field of ethics, and it is this Platonic Socrates who also lends his name to the concepts of Socratic irony and the Socratic method, or elenchus. The latter remains a commonly used tool in a wide range of discussions, and is a type of pedagogy in which a series of questions are asked not only to draw individual answers, but also to encourage fundamental insight into the issue at hand. It is Plato's Socrates that also made important and lasting contributions to the fields of epistemology and logic, and the influence of his ideas and approach remains strong in providing a foundation for much western philosophy that followed.

As one recent commentator has put it, Plato, the idealist, offers "an idol, a master figure, for philosophy. A Saint, a prophet of the 'Sun-God', a teacher condemned for his teachings as a heretic." Yet, the 'real' Socrates, like many of the other ancient philosophers, remains, at best, enigmatic and, at worst, unknown.

A system of morality which is based on relative emotional values is a mere illusion, a thoroughly vulgar conception which has nothing sound in it and nothing true. All men's souls are immortal, but the souls of the righteous are immortal and divine.
Socrates

An honest man is always a child.
Socrates

As for me, all I know is that I know nothing.
Socrates

**As to marriage or celibacy, let a man take which course
he will, he will be sure to repent.**
Socrates

Be as you wish to seem.
Socrates

**Be slow to fall into friendship; but when thou art in,
continue firm and constant.**
Socrates

Beauty is a short-lived tyranny.
Socrates

**Beauty is the bait which with delight allures man to
enlarge his kind.**
Socrates

Beware the barrenness of a busy life.
Socrates

**By all means, marry. If you get a good wife, you'll
become happy; if you get a bad one, you'll become a
philosopher.**
Socrates

Death may be the greatest of all human blessings.
Socrates

Employ your time in improving yourself by other men's writings, so that you shall gain easily what others have labored hard for.
Socrates

False words are not only evil in themselves, but they infect the soul with evil.
Socrates

From the deepest desires often come the deadliest hate.
Socrates

He is a man of courage who does not run away, but remains at his post and fights against the enemy.
Socrates

He is richest who is content with the least, for content is the wealth of nature.
Socrates

I am the wisest man alive, for I know one thing, and that is that I know nothing.
Socrates

I decided that it was not wisdom that enabled poets to write their poetry, but a kind of instinct or inspiration, such as you find in seers and prophets who deliver all their sublime messages without knowing in the least what they mean.
Socrates

I know nothing except the fact of my ignorance.
Socrates

I know that I am intelligent, because I know that I know nothing.
Socrates

I only wish that ordinary people had an unlimited capacity for doing harm; then they might have an unlimited power for doing good.
Socrates

I was really too honest a man to be a politician and live.
Socrates

If a man is proud of his wealth, he should not be praised until it is known how he employs it.
Socrates

If all misfortunes were laid in one common heap whence everyone must take an equal portion, most people would be contented to take their own and depart.
Socrates

It is not living that matters, but living rightly.
Socrates

Let him that would move the world first move himself.
Socrates

My advice to you is get married: if you find a good wife you'll be happy; if not, you'll become a philosopher.
Socrates

Not life, but good life, is to be chiefly valued.
Socrates

Once made equal to man, woman becomes his superior.
Socrates

One who is injured ought not to return the injury, for on no account can it be right to do an injustice; and it is not right to return an injury, or to do evil to any man, however much we have suffered from him.
Socrates

Ordinary people seem not to realize that those who really apply themselves in the right way to philosophy are directly and of their own accord preparing themselves for dying and death.
Socrates

Our prayers should be for blessings in general, for God knows best what is good for us.
Socrates

The end of life is to be like God, and the soul following God will be like Him.
Socrates

The greatest way to live with honor in this world is to be what we pretend to be.
Socrates

The only true wisdom is in knowing you know nothing.
Socrates

The poets are only the interpreters of the Gods.
Socrates

The unexamined life is not worth living.
Socrates

The way to gain a good reputation is to endeavor to be what you desire to appear.
Socrates

To know, is to know that you know nothing. That is the meaning of true knowledge.
Socrates

True knowledge exists in knowing that you know nothing.
Socrates

True wisdom comes to each of us when we realize how little we understand about life, ourselves, and the world around us.
Socrates

Where there is reverence there is fear, but there is not reverence everywhere that there is fear, because fear presumably has a wider extension than reverence.
Socrates

Wisdom begins in wonder.
Socrates

Worthless people live only to eat and drink; people of worth eat and drink only to live.
Socrates

Plato
(429–347 B.C.E.)

Plato was a Classical Greek philosopher, mathematician, student of Socrates, writer of philosophical dialogues, and founder of the Academy in Athens, the first institution of higher learning in the Western world. Along with his mentor, Socrates, and his student, Aristotle, Plato helped to lay the foundations of Western philosophy and science.

Plato's sophistication as a writer is evident in his Socratic dialogues; thirty-six dialogues and thirteen letters have been ascribed to him. Plato's writings have been published in several fashions; this has led to several conventions regarding the naming and referencing of Plato's texts.

Plato's dialogues have been used to teach a range of subjects, including philosophy, logic, ethics, rhetoric, and mathematics.

Excerpt from BOOK IV - LAWS:

I was going to make the saddening reflection, that accidents of all sorts are the true legislators,—wars and pestilences and famines and the frequent recurrence of bad seasons. The observer will be inclined to say that almost all human things are chance; and this is certainly true about navigation and medicine, and the art of the general.

But there is another thing which may equally be said. 'What is it?'

That God governs all things, and that chance and opportunity co-operate with Him. And according to yet a third view, art has part with them, for surely in a storm it is well to have a pilot? And the same is true of legislation: even if circumstances are favourable, a skilful lawgiver is still necessary.

'Most true.' All artists would pray for certain conditions under which to exercise their art: and would not the legislator do the same?

'Certainly?' Come, legislator, let us say to him, and what are the conditions which you would have?

He will answer, Grant me a city which is ruled by a tyrant; and let the tyrant be young, mindful, teachable, courageous, magnanimous; and let him have the inseparable condition of all virtue, which is temperance—not prudence, but that natural temperance which is the gift of children and animals, and is hardly reckoned among goods—with this he must be endowed, if the state is to acquire the form most conducive to happiness in the speediest manner.

And I must add one other condition: the tyrant must be fortunate, and his good fortune must consist in his having the co-operation of a great legislator. When God has done all this, He has done the best which He can for a state; not so well if He has given them two legislators instead of one, and less and less well if He has given them a great many.

An orderly tyranny most easily passes into the perfect state; in the second degree, a monarchy; in the third degree, a democracy; an oligarchy is worst of all. 'I do not understand.' I suppose that you have never seen a city which is subject to a tyranny? 'I have no desire to see one.' You would have seen what I am describing, if you ever had.

The tyrant can speedily change the manners of a state, and affix the stamp of praise or blame on any action which he pleases; for the citizens readily follow the example which he sets. There is no quicker way of making changes; but there is a counterbalancing difficulty.

It is hard to find the divine love of temperance and justice existing in any powerful form of government, whether in a monarchy or an oligarchy.

In olden days there were chiefs like Nestor, who was the most eloquent and temperate of mankind, but there is no one his equal now.

If such an one ever arises among us, blessed will he be, and blessed they who listen to his words. For where power and wisdom and temperance meet in one, there are the best laws and constitutions. I am endeavouring to show you how easy under the conditions supposed, and how difficult under any other, is the task of giving a city good laws. 'How do you mean?'

Let us old men attempt to mould in words a constitution for your new state, as children make figures out of wax. 'Proceed. What constitution shall we give—democracy, oligarchy, or aristocracy?' To which of these classes, Megillus, do you refer your own state? 'The Spartan constitution seems to me to contain all these elements.

Our state is a democracy and also an aristocracy; the power of the Ephors is tyrannical, and we have an ancient monarchy.' 'Much the same,' adds Cleinias, 'may be said of Cnosus.'

The reason is that you have polities, but other states are mere aggregations of men dwelling together, which are named after their several ruling powers; whereas a state, if an 'ocracy' at all, should be called a theocracy.

A tale of old will explain my meaning. There is a tradition of a golden age, in which all things were spontaneous and abundant. Cronos, then lord of the world, knew that no mortal nature could endure the temptations of power, and therefore he appointed demons or demi-gods, who are of a superior race, to have dominion over man, as man has dominion over the animals.

They took care of us with great ease and pleasure to themselves, and no less to us; and the tradition says that only when God, and not man, is the ruler, can the human race cease from ill.

This was the manner of life which prevailed under Cronos, and which we must strive to follow so far as the principle of immortality still abides in us and we live according to law and the dictates of right reason.

But in an oligarchy or democracy, when the governing principle is athirst for pleasure, the laws are trampled under foot, and there is no possibility of salvation. Is it not often said that there are as many forms of laws as there are governments, and that they have no concern either with any one virtue or with all virtue, but are relative to the will of the government? Which is as much as to say that 'might makes right.'

'What do you mean?' I mean that governments enact their own laws, and that every government makes self-preservation its principal aim. He who transgresses the laws is regarded as an evil-doer, and punished accordingly. This was one of the unjust principles of government which we mentioned when speaking of the different claims to rule.

We were agreed that parents should rule their children, the elder the younger, the noble the ignoble. But there were also several other principles, and among them Pindar's 'law of violence.' To whom then is our state to be entrusted?

For many a government is only a victorious faction which has a monopoly of power, and refuses any share to the conquered, lest when they get into office they should remember their wrongs. Such governments are not polities, but parties; nor are any laws good which are made in the interest of particular classes only, and not of the whole.

And in our state I mean to protest against making any man a ruler because he is rich, or strong, or noble. But those who are obedient to the laws, and who win the victory of obedience, shall be promoted to the service of the Gods according to the degree of their obedience.

When I call the ruler the servant or minister of the law, this is not a mere paradox, but I mean to say that upon a willingness to obey the law the existence of the state depends. 'Truly, Stranger, you have a keen vision.' Why, yes; every man when he is old has his intellectual vision most keen.

And now shall we call in our colonists and make a speech to them? Friends, we say to them, God holds in His hand the beginning, middle, and end of all things, and He moves in a straight line towards the accomplishment of His will. Justice always bears Him company, and punishes those who fall short of His laws.

He who would be happy follows humbly in her train; but he who is lifted up with pride, or wealth, or honour, or beauty, is soon deserted by God, and, being deserted, he lives in confusion and disorder. To many he seems a great man; but in a short time he comes to utter destruction. Wherefore, seeing these things, what ought we to do or think? 'Every man ought to follow God.' What life, then, is pleasing to God? There is an old saying that 'like agrees with like, measure with measure,' and God ought to be our measure in all things.

The temperate man is the friend of God because he is like Him, and the intemperate man is not His friend, because he is not like Him. And the conclusion is, that the best of all things for a good man is to pray and sacrifice to the Gods; but the bad man has a polluted soul; and therefore his service is wasted upon the Gods, while the good are accepted of them.

I have told you the mark at which we ought to aim. You will say, How, and with what weapons? In the first place we affirm, that after the Olympian Gods and the Gods of the state, honour should be given to the Gods below, and to them should be offered everything in even numbers and of the second choice; the auspicious odd numbers and everything of the first choice are reserved for the Gods above.

Next demi-gods or spirits must be honoured, and then heroes, and after them family gods, who will be worshipped at their local seats according to law. Further, the honour due to parents should not be forgotten; children owe all that they have to them, and the debt must be repaid by kindness and attention in old age.

No unbecoming word must be uttered before them; for there is an avenging angel who hears them when they are angry, and the child should consider that the parent when he has been wronged has a right to be angry. After their death let them have a moderate funeral, such as their fathers have had before them; and there shall be an annual commemoration of them.

Living on this wise, we shall be accepted of the Gods, and shall pass our days in good hope. The law will determine all our various duties towards relatives and friends and other citizens, and the whole state will be happy and prosperous.

But if the legislator would persuade as well as command, he will add prefaces to his laws which will predispose the citizens to virtue. Even a little accomplished in the way of gaining the hearts of men is of great value. For most men are in no particular haste to become good.

Patañjali
(200 and 400 AD)

Patañjali is the compiler of the Yoga Sūtras, an important collection of aphorisms on Yoga practice. According to tradition, the same Patañjali was also the author of the Mahābhāya, a commentary on Kātyāyana's vārttikas (short comments) on Pāini's Aādhyāyī as well as an unspecified work of medicine (āyurveda). In recent decades the Yoga Sutra has become quite popular worldwide for the precepts regarding practice of Raja Yoga and its philosophical basis. "Yoga" in traditional Hinduism involves inner contemplation, a system of meditation practice and ethics.

"When you are inspired by some great purpose, some extraordinary project, all your thoughts break their bonds: Your mind transcends limitations, your consciousness expands in every direction, and you find yourself in a new, great, and wonderful world. Dormant forces, faculties and talents become alive, and your discover yourself to be a greater person by far than you ever dreamed yourself to be."

"Peace can be reached through meditation on the knowledge which dreams give. Peace can also be reached through concentration upon that which is dearest to the heart."

"When a gifted team dedicates itself to unselfish trust and combines instinct with boldness and effort, it is ready to climb."

"In deep meditation the flow of concentration is continuous like the flow of oil."

"When a man becomes steadfast in his abstention from harming others, then all living creatures will cease to feel enmity in his presence"

Excerpt from THE YOGA SUTRAS OF PATANJALI
"The Book of the Spiritual Man"

BOOK I

1. OM: Here follows Instruction in Union.

Union, here as always i4n the Scriptures of India, means union of the individual soul with the Oversoul; of the personal consciousness with the Divine Consciousness, whereby the mortal becomes immortal, and enters the Eternal. Therefore, salvation is, first, freedom from sin and the sorrow which comes from sin, and then a divine and eternal well-being, wherein the soul partakes of the being, the wisdom and glory of God.

2. Union, spiritual consciousness, is gained through control of the versatile psychic nature.

The goal is the full consciousness of the spiritual man, illumined by the Divine Light. Nothing except the obdurate resistance of the psychic nature keeps us back from the goal. The psychical powers are spiritual powers run wild, perverted, drawn from their proper channel. Therefore our first task is, to regain control of this perverted nature, to chasten, purify and restore the misplaced powers.

3. Then the Seer comes to consciousness in his proper nature.

Egotism is but the perversion of spiritual being. Ambition is the inversion of spiritual power. Passion is the distortion of love. The mortal is the limitation of the immortal. When these false images give place to true, then the spiritual man stands forth luminous, as the sun, when the clouds disperse.

4. Heretofore the Seer has been enmeshed in the activities of the psychic nature.

The power and life which are the heritage of the spiritual man have been caught and enmeshed in psychical activities. Instead of pure being in the Divine, there has been fretful, combative, egotism, its hand against every man. Instead of the light of pure vision, there have been restless senses nave been re and imaginings. Instead of spiritual joy, the undivided joy of pure being, there has been self-indulgence of body and mind. These are all real forces, but distorted from their true nature and goal. They must be extricated, like gems from the matrix, like the pith from the reed, steadily, without destructive violence. Spiritual powers are to be drawn forth from the psychic meshes.

5. The psychic activities are five; they are either subject or not subject to the five hindrances (Book II, 3).

The psychic nature is built up through the image-making power, the power which lies behind and dwells in mind-pictures. These pictures do not remain quiescent in the mind; they are kinetic, restless, stimulating to new acts. Thus the mind-image of an indulgence suggests and invites to a new indulgence; the picture of past joy is framed in regrets or hopes. And there is the ceaseless play of the desire to know, to penetrate to the essence of things, to classify. This, too, busies itself ceaselessly with the mind-images. So that we may classify the activities of the psychic nature thus:

6. These activities are: Sound intellection, unsound intellection, predication, sleep, memory.

We have here a list of mental and emotional powers; of powers that picture and observe, and of powers that picture and feel. But the power to know and feel is spiritual and immortal. What is needed is, not to destroy it, but to raise it from the psychical to the spiritual realm.

7. The elements of sound intellection are: direct observation, inductive reason, and trustworthy testimony.

Each of these is a spiritual power, thinly veiled. Direct observation is the outermost form of the Soul's pure vision. Inductive reason rests on the great principles of continuity and correspondence; and these, on the supreme truth that all life is of the One. Trustworthy testimony, the sharing of one soul in the wisdom of another, rests on the ultimate oneness of all souls.

8. Unsound intellection is false understanding, not resting on a perception of the true nature of things.

When the object is not truly perceived, when the observation is inaccurate and faulty, thought or reasoning based on that mistaken perception is of necessity false and unsound.

9. Predication is carried on through words or thoughts not resting on an object perceived.

The purpose of this Sutra is, to distinguish between the mental process of predication, and observation, induction or testimony. Predication is the attribution of a quality or action to a subject, by adding to it a predicate. In the sentence, "the man is wise," "the man" is the subject; "is wise" is the predicate. This may be simply an interplay of thoughts, without the presence of the object thought of; or the things thought of may be imaginary or unreal; while observation, induction and testimony always go back to an object.

10. Sleep is the psychic condition which rests on mind states, all material things being absent.

In waking life, we have two currents of perception; an outer current of physical things seen and heard and perceived; an inner current of mind-images and thoughts. The outer current ceases in sleep; the inner current continues, and watching the mind-images float before the field of consciousness, we "dream." Even when there are no dreams, there is still a certain consciousness in sleep, so that, on waking, one says, "I have slept well," or "I have slept badly."

11. Memory is holding to mind-images of things perceived, without modifying them.

Here, as before, the mental power is explained in terms of mind-images, which are the material of which the psychic world is built,

Therefore the sages teach that the world of our perception, which is indeed a world of mind-images, is but the wraith or shadow of the real and everlasting world. In this sense, memory is but the psychical inversion of the spiritual, ever-present vision. That which is ever before the spiritual eye of the Seer needs not to be remembered.

12. The control of these psychic activities comes through the right use of the will, and through ceasing from self-indulgence.

If these psychical powers and energies, even such evil things as passion and hate and fear, are but spiritual powers fallen and perverted, how are we to bring about their release and restoration? Two means are presented to us: the awakening of the spiritual will, and the purification of mind and thought.

13. The right use of the will is the steady, effort to stand in spiritual being.

We have thought of ourselves, perhaps, as creatures moving upon this earth, rather helpless, at the mercy of storm and hunger and our enemies. We are to think of ourselves as immortals, dwelling in the Light, encompassed and sustained by spiritual powers. The steady effort to hold this thought will awaken dormant and unrealized powers, which will unveil to us the nearness of the Eternal.

14. This becomes a firm resting-place, when followed long, persistently, with earnestness.

We must seek spiritual life in conformity with the laws of spiritual life, with earnestness, humility, gentle charity, which is an acknowledgment of the One Soul within us all. Only through obedience to that shared Life, through perpetual remembrance of our oneness with all Divine Being, our nothingness apart from Divine Being, can we enter our inheritance.

15. Ceasing from self-indulgence is conscious mastery over the thirst for sensuous pleasure here or hereafter.

Rightly understood, the desire for sensation is the desire of being, the distortion of the soul's eternal life. The lust of sensual stimulus and excitation rests on the longing to feel one's life keenly, to gain the sense of being really alive. This sense of true life comes only with the coming of the soul, and the soul comes only in silence, after self-indulgence has been courageously and loyally stilled, through reverence before the coming soul.

16. The consummation of this is freedom from thirst for any mode of psychical activity, through the establishment of the spiritual man.

In order to gain a true understanding of this teaching, study must be supplemented by devoted practice, faith by works. The reading of the words will not avail. There must be a real effort to stand as the Soul, a real ceasing from self-indulgence. With this awakening of the spiritual will, and purification, will come at once the growth of the spiritual man and our awakening consciousness as the spiritual man; and this, attained in even a small degree, will help us notably in our contest. To him that hath, shall be given.

17. Meditation with an object follows these stages: first, exterior examining, then interior judicial action, then joy, then realization of individual being.

In the practice of meditation, a beginning may be made by fixing the attention upon some external object, such as a sacred image or picture, or a part of a book of devotion. In the second stage, one passes from the outer object to an inner pondering upon its lessons. The third stage is the inspiration, the heightening of the spiritual will, which results from this pondering. The fourth stage is the realization of one's spiritual being, as enkindled by this meditation.

18. After the exercise of the will has stilled the psychic activities, meditation rests only on the fruit of former meditations.

In virtue of continued practice and effort, the need of an external object on which to rest the meditation is outgrown. An interior state of spiritual consciousness is reached, which is called "the cloud of things knowable" (Book IV, 29).

19. Subjective consciousness arising from a natural cause is possessed by those who have laid aside their bodies and been absorbed into subjective nature.

Those who have died, entered the paradise between births, are in a condition resembling meditation without an external object. But in the fullness of time, the seeds of desire in them will spring up, and they will be born again into this world.

20. For the others, there is spiritual consciousness, led up to by faith, valour right mindfulness, one-pointedness, perception.

It is well to keep in mind these steps on the path to illumination: faith, valour, right mindfulness, one-pointedness, perception. Not one can be dispensed with; all must be won. First faith; and then from faith, valour; from valour, right mindfulness; from right mindfulness, a one-pointed aspiration toward the soul; from this, perception; and finally, full vision as the soul.

21. Spiritual consciousness is nearest to those of keen, intense will.

The image used is the swift impetus of the torrent; the kingdom must be taken by force. Firm will comes only through effort; effort is inspired by faith. The great secret is this: it is not enough to have intuitions; we must act on them; we must live them.

22. The will may be weak, or of middle strength, or intense.

Therefore there is a spiritual consciousness higher than this. For those of weak will, there is this counsel: to be faithful in obedience, to live the life, and thus to strengthen the will to more perfect obedience. The will is not ours, but God's, and we come into it only through obedience. As we enter into the spirit of God, we are permitted to share the power of God.

Higher than the three stages of the way is the goal, the end of the way.

23. Or spiritual consciousness may be gained by ardent service of the Master.

If we think of our lives as tasks laid on us by the Master of Life, if we look on all duties as parts of that Master's work, entrusted to us, and forming our life-work; then, if we obey, promptly, loyally, sincerely, we shall enter by degrees into the Master's life and share the Master's power. Thus we shall be initiated into the spiritual will.

24. The Master is the spiritual man, who is free from hindrances, bondage to works, and the fruition and seed of works.

The Soul of the Master, the Lord, is of the same nature as the soul in us; but we still bear the burden of many evils, we are in bondage through our former works, we are under the dominance of sorrow. The Soul of the Master is free from sin and servitude and sorrow.

25. In the Master is the perfect seed of Omniscience.

The Soul of the Master is in essence one with the Oversoul, and therefore partaker of the Oversoul's all-wisdom and all-power. All spiritual attainment rests on this, and is possible because the soul and the Oversoul are One.

26. He is the Teacher of all who have gone before, since he is not limited by Time.

From the beginning, the Oversoul has been the Teacher of all souls, which, by their entrance into the Oversoul, by realizing their oneness with the Oversoul, have inherited the kingdom of the Light. For the Oversoul is before Time, and Time, father of all else, is one of His children.

27. His word is OM.

OM: the symbol of the Three in One, the three worlds in the Soul; the three times, past, present, future, in Eternity; the three Divine Powers, Creation, Preservation, Transformation, in the one Being; the three essences, immortality, omniscience, joy, in the one Spirit. This is the

Word, the Symbol, of the Master and Lord, the perfected Spiritual Man.

28. Let there be soundless repetition of OM and meditation thereon.

This has many meanings, in ascending degrees. There is, first, the potency of the word itself, as of all words. Then there is the manifold significance of the symbol, as suggested above. Lastly, there is the spiritual realization of the high essences thus symbolized. Thus we rise step by step to the Eternal.

29. Thence come the awakening of interior consciousness, and the removal of barriers.

Here again faith must be supplemented by works, the life must be led as well as studied, before the full meaning can be understood. The awakening of spiritual consciousness can only be understood in measure as it is entered. It can only be entered where the conditions are present: purity of heart, and strong aspiration, and the resolute conquest of each sin.

This, however, may easily be understood: that the recognition of the three worlds as resting in the Soul leads us to realize ourselves and all life as of the Soul; that, as we dwell, not in past, present or future, but in the Eternal, we become more at one with the Eternal; that, as we view all organization, preservation, mutation as the work of the Divine One, we shall come more into harmony with the One, and thus remove the barrier' in our path toward the Light.

In the second part of the first book, the problem of the emergence of the spiritual man is further dealt with. We are led to the consideration of the barriers to his emergence, of the overcoming of the barriers, and of certain steps and stages in the ascent from the ordinary consciousness of practical life, to the finer, deeper, radiant consciousness of the spiritual man.

30. The barriers to interior consciousness, which drive the psychic nature this way and that, are these: sickness, inertia, doubt, lightmindedness, laziness, intemperance, false notions, inability to reach a stage of meditation, or to hold it when reached.

We must remember that we are considering the spiritual man as enwrapped and enmeshed by the psychic nature, the emotional and mental powers; and as unable to come to clear consciousness, unable to stand and see clearly, because of the psychic veils of the personality. Nine of these are enumerated, and they go pretty thoroughly into the brute toughness of the psychic nature.

Sickness is included rather for its effect on the emotions and mind, since bodily infirmity, such as blindness or deafness, is no insuperable barrier to spiritual life, and may sometimes be a help, as cutting off distractions. It will be well for us to ponder over each of these nine activities, thinking of each as a psychic state, a barrier to the interior consciousness of the spiritual man.

31. Grieving, despondency, bodily restlessness, the drawing in and sending forth of the life-breath also contribute to drive the psychic nature to and fro.

The first two moods are easily understood. We can well see bow a sodden psychic condition, flagrantly opposed to the pure and positive joy of spiritual life, would be a barrier. The next, bodily restlessness, is in a special way the fault of our day and generation. When it is conquered, mental restlessness will be half conquered, too.

The next two terms, concerning the life breath, offer some difficulty. The surface meaning is harsh and irregular breathing; the deeper meaning is a life of harsh and irregular impulses.

32. Steady application to a principle is the way to put a stop to these.

The will, which, in its pristine state, was full of vigour, has been steadily corrupted by self-indulgence, the seeking of moods and sensations for sensation's sake. Hence come all the morbid and sickly moods of the mind. The remedy is a return to the pristine state of the will, by vigorous, positive effort; or, as we are here told, by steady application to a principle. The principle to which we should thus steadily apply ourselves should be one arising from the reality of spiritual life; valorous work for the soul, in others as in ourselves.

33. By sympathy with the happy, compassion for the sorrowful, delight in the holy, disregard of the unholy, the psychic nature moves to gracious peace.

When we are wrapped up in ourselves, shrouded with the cloak of our egotism, absorbed in our pains and bitter thoughts, we are not willing to disturb or strain our own sickly mood by giving kindly sympathy to the happy, thus doubling their joy, or by showing compassion for the sad, thus halving their sorrow. We refuse to find delight in holy things, and let the mind brood in sad pessimism on unholy things. All these evil psychic moods must be conquered by strong effort of will. This rending of the veils will reveal to us something of the grace and peace which are of the interior consciousness of the spiritual man.

34. Or peace may be reached by the even sending forth and control of the life-breath.

Here again we may look for a double meaning: first, that even and quiet breathing which is a part of the victory over bodily restlessness; then the even and quiet tenor of life, without harsh or dissonant impulses, which brings stillness to the heart.

35. Faithful, persistent application to any object, if completely attained, will bind the mind to steadiness.

We are still considering how to overcome the wavering and perturbation of the psychic nature, which make it quite unfit to transmit the inward consciousness and stillness. We are once more told to use the will, and to train it by steady and persistent work: by "sitting close" to our work, in the phrase of the original.

36. As also will a joyful, radiant spirit.

There is no such illusion as gloomy pessimism, and it has been truly said that a man's cheerfulness is the measure of his faith. Gloom, despondency, the pale cast of thought, are very amenable to the will. Sturdy and courageous effort will bring a clear and valorous mind. But it must always be remembered that this is not for solace to the personal man, but is rather an offering to the ideal of spiritual life, a contribution to the universal and universally shared treasure in heaven.

37. Or the purging of self-indulgence from the psychic nature.

We must recognize that the fall of man is a reality, exemplified in our own persons. We have quite other sins than the animals, and far more deleterious; and they have all come through self-indulgence, with which our psychic natures are soaked through and through. As we climbed down hill for our pleasure, so must we climb up again for our purification and restoration to our former high estate. The process is painful, perhaps, yet indispensable.

38. Or a pondering on the perceptions gained in dreams and dreamless sleep.

For the Eastern sages, dreams are, it is true, made up of images of waking life, reflections of what the eyes have seen and the ears heard. But dreams are something more, for the images are in a sense real, objective on their own plane; and the knowledge that there is another world, even a dream-world, lightens the tyranny of material life. Much of poetry and art is such a solace from dreamland. But there is more in dream, for it may image what is above, as well as what is below; not only the children of men, but also the children by the shore of the immortal sea that brought us hither, may throw their images on this magic mirror: so, too, of the secrets of dreamless sleep with its pure vision, in even greater degree.

39. Or meditative brooding on what is dearest to the heart.

Here is a thought which our own day is beginning to grasp: that love is a form of knowledge; that we truly know any thing or any person, by becoming one therewith, in love. Thus love has a wisdom that the mind cannot claim, and by this hearty love, this becoming one with what is beyond our personal borders, we may take a long step toward freedom. Two directions for this may be suggested: the pure love of the artist for his work, and the earnest, compassionate search into the hearts of others.

40. Thus he masters all, from the atom to the Infinite.

Newton was asked how he made his discoveries. By intending my mind on them, he replied. This steady pressure, this becoming one with what we seek to understand, whether it be atom or soul, is the one means to know. When we become a thing, we really know it, not otherwise. Therefore live the life, to know the doctrine; do the will of the Father, if you would know the Father.

41. When the perturbations of the psychic nature have all been stilled, then the consciousness, like a pure crystal, takes the colour of what it rests on, whether that be the perceiver, perceiving, or the thing perceived.

This is a fuller expression of the last Sutra, and is so lucid that comment can hardly add to it. Everything is either perceiver, perceiving, or the thing perceived; or, as we might say, consciousness, force, or matter. The sage tells us that the one key will unlock the secrets of all three, the secrets of consciousness, force and matter alike. The thought is, that the cordial sympathy of a gentle heart, intuitively understanding the hearts of others, is really a manifestation of the same power as that penetrating perception whereby one divines the secrets of planetary motions or atomic structure.

42. When the consciousness, poised in perceiving, blends together the name, the object dwelt on and the idea, this is perception with exterior consideration.

In the first stage of the consideration of an external object, the perceiving mind comes to it, preoccupied by the name and idea conventionally associated with that object. For example, in coming to the study of a book, we think of the author, his period, the school to which he belongs. The second stage, set forth in the next Sutra, goes directly to the spiritual meaning of the book, setting its traditional trappings aside and finding its application to our own experience and problems.

The commentator takes a very simple illustration: a cow, where one considers, in the first stage, the name of the cow, the animal itself and the idea of a cow in the mind. In the second stage, one pushes these trappings aside and, entering into the inmost being of the cow, shares its consciousness, as do some of the artists who paint cows. They get at the very life of what they study and paint.

43. When the object dwells in the mind, clear of memory-pictures, uncoloured by the mind, as a pure luminous idea, this is perception without exterior or consideration.

We are still considering external, visible objects. Such perception as is here described is of the nature of that penetrating vision whereby Newton, intending his mind on things, made his discoveries, or that whereby a really great portrait painter pierces to the soul of him whom he paints, and makes that soul live on canvas. These stages of perception are described in this way, to lead the mind up to an understanding of the piercing soul-vision of the spiritual man, the immortal.

44. The same two steps, when referring to things of finer substance, are said to be with, or without, judicial action of the mind.

We now come to mental or psychical objects: to images in the mind. It is precisely by comparing, arranging and superposing these mind-images that we get our general notions or concepts. This process of analysis and synthesis, whereby we select certain qualities in a group of mind-images, and then range together those of like quality, is the judicial action of the mind spoken of. But when we exercise swift divination upon the mind images, as does a poet or a man of genius, then we use a power higher than the judicial, and one nearer to the keen vision of the spiritual man.

45. Subtle substance rises in ascending degrees, to that pure nature which has no distinguishing mark.

As we ascend from outer material things which are permeated by separateness, and whose chief characteristic is to be separate, just as so many pebbles are separate from each other; as we ascend, first, to mind-images, which overlap and coalesce in both space and time, and then to ideas and principles, we finally come to purer essences, drawing ever nearer and nearer to unity.

Or we may illustrate this principle thus. Our bodily, external selves are quite distinct and separate, in form, name, place, substance; our mental selves, of finer substance, meet and part, meet and part again, in perpetual concussion and interchange; our spiritual selves attain true consciousness through unity, where the partition wall between us and the Highest, between us and others, is broken down and we are all made perfect in the One. The highest riches are possessed by all pure souls, only when united. Thus we rise from separation to true individuality in unity.

46. The above are the degrees of limited and conditioned spiritual consciousness, still containing the seed of separateness.

In the four stages of perception above described, the spiritual vision is still working through the mental and psychical, the inner genius is still expressed through the outer, personal man. The spiritual man has yet to come completely to consciousness as himself, in his own realm, the psychical veils laid aside.

47. When pure perception without judicial action of the mind is reached, there follows the gracious peace of the inner self.

We have instanced certain types of this pure perception: the poet's divination, whereby he sees the spirit within the symbol, likeness in things unlike, and beauty in all things; the pure insight of the true philosopher, whose vision rests not on the appearances of life, but on its realities; or the saint's firm perception of spiritual life and being. All these are far advanced on the way; they have drawn near to the secret dwelling of peace.

48. In that peace, perception is unfailingly true.

The poet, the wise philosopher and the saint not only reach a wide and luminous consciousness, but they gain certain knowledge of substantial reality. When we know, we know that we know. For we have come to the stage where we know things by being them, and nothing can be more true than being. We rest on the rock, and know it to be rock, rooted in the very heart of the world.

49. The object of this perception is other than what is learned from the sacred books, or by sound inference, since this perception is particular.

The distinction is a luminous and inspiring one. The Scriptures teach general truths, concerning universal spiritual life and broad laws, and inference from their teaching is not less general. But the spiritual perception of the awakened Seer brings particular truth concerning his own particular life and needs, whether these be for himself or others. He receives defined, precise knowledge, exactly applying to what he has at heart.

50. The impress on the consciousness springing from this perception supersedes all previous impressions.

Each state or field of the mind, each field of knowledge, so to speak, which is reached by mental and emotional energies, is a psychical state, just as the mind picture of a stage with the actors on it, is a psychical state or field. When the pure vision, as of the poet, the philosopher, the saint, fills the whole field, all lesser views and visions are crowded out. This high consciousness displaces all lesser consciousness. Yet, in a certain sense, that which is viewed as part, even by the vision of a sage, has still an element of illusion, a thin psychical veil, however pure and luminous that veil may be. It is the last and highest psychic state.

51. When this impression ceases, then, since all impressions have ceased, there arises pure spiritual consciousness, with no seed of separateness left.

The last psychic veil is drawn aside, and the spiritual man stands with unveiled vision, pure serene.

Buddha
(563 B.C.E.-483 B.C.E.)

Siddhārtha Gautama Pali: Siddhattha Gotama was a spiritual teacher who founded Buddhism. In most Buddhist traditions, he is regarded as the Supreme Buddha of our age, "Buddha" meaning "awakened one" or "the enlightened one." The time of his birth and death are uncertain: most early 20th-century historians dated his lifetime as c. 563 BCE to 483 BCE, but more recent opinion dates his death to between 486 and 483 BCE or, according to some, between 411 and 400 BCE. By tradition, Gautama is said to have been born in the small state of Kapilavastu, in what is now Nepal, and later to have taught primarily throughout regions of eastern India such as Magadha and Kośala.

Gautama, also known as Śākyamuni ("Sage of the Śākyas"), is the primary figure in Buddhism, and accounts of his life, discourses, and monastic rules are believed by Buddhists to have been summarized after his death and memorized by his followers. Various collections of teachings attributed to him were passed down by oral tradition, and first committed to writing about 400 years later.

He is also regarded as a god or prophet in other world religions or denominations, including Hinduism, Ahmadiyya Islam and the Bahá'í faith.

All that we are is the result of what we have thought. If a man speaks or acts with an evil thought, pain follows him. If a man speaks or acts with a pure thought, happiness follows him, like a shadow that never leaves him.
Buddha

All wrong-doing arises because of mind. If mind is transformed can wrong-doing remain?
Buddha

An insincere and evil friend is more to be feared than a wild beast; a wild beast may wound your body, but an evil friend will wound your mind.
Buddha

Better than a thousand hollow words, is one word that brings peace.
Buddha

Chaos is inherent in all compounded things. Strive on with diligence.
Buddha

Do not dwell in the past, do not dream of the future, concentrate the mind on the present moment.
Buddha

Do not overrate what you have received, nor envy others. He who envies others does not obtain peace of mind.
Buddha

Even death is not to be feared by one who has lived wisely.
Buddha

Hatred does not cease by hatred, but only by love; this is the eternal rule.
Buddha

He who loves 50 people has 50 woes; he who loves no one has no woes.
Buddha

Health is the greatest gift, contentment the greatest wealth,
faithfulness the best relationship.
Buddha

Holding on to anger is like grasping a hot coal with the
intent of throwing it at someone else; you are the one who
gets burned.
Buddha

However many holy words you read, however many you
speak, what good will they do you if you do not act on upon
them?
Buddha

I do not believe in a fate that falls on men however they act;
but I do believe in a fate that falls on them unless they act.
Buddha

I never see what has been done; I only see what remains to
be done.
Buddha

In a controversy the instant we feel anger we have already
ceased striving for the truth, and have begun striving for
ourselves.
Buddha

In the sky, there is no distinction of east and west; people
create distinctions out of their own minds and then believe
them to be true.
Buddha

It is a man's own mind, not his enemy or foe, that lures him to evil ways.
Buddha

It is better to conquer yourself than to win a thousand battles. Then the victory is yours. It cannot be taken from you, not by angels or by demons, heaven or hell.
Buddha

It is better to travel well than to arrive.
Buddha

Just as a candle cannot burn without fire, men cannot live without a spiritual life.
Buddha

Just as treasures are uncovered from the earth, so virtue appears from good deeds, and wisdom appears from a pure and peaceful mind. To walk safely through the maze of human life, one needs the light of wisdom and the guidance of virtue.
Buddha

No one saves us but ourselves. No one can and no one may. We ourselves must walk the path.
Buddha

Peace comes from within. Do not seek it without.
Buddha

The foot feels the foot when it feels the ground.
Buddha

The mind is everything. What you think you become.
Buddha

The only real failure in life is not to be true to the best one knows.
Buddha

The tongue like a sharp knife... Kills without drawing blood.
Buddha

The virtues, like the Muses, are always seen in groups. A good principle was never found solitary in any breast.
Buddha

The way is not in the sky. The way is in the heart.
Buddha

The whole secret of existence is to have no fear. Never fear what will become of you, depend on no one. Only the moment you reject all help are you freed.
Buddha

The wise ones fashioned speech with their thought, sifting it as grain is sifted through a sieve.
Buddha

There are only two mistakes one can make along the road to truth; not going all the way, and not starting.
Buddha

There has to be evil so that good can prove its purity above it.
Buddha

There is nothing more dreadful than the habit of doubt. Doubt separates people. It is a poison that disintegrates friendships and breaks up pleasant relations. It is a thorn that irritates and hurts; it is a sword that kills.
Buddha

Those who are free of resentful thoughts surely find peace.
Buddha

Three things cannot be long hidden: the sun, the moon, and the truth.
Buddha

To be idle is a short road to death and to be diligent is a way of life; foolish people are idle, wise people are diligent.
Buddha

To enjoy good health, to bring true happiness to one's family, to bring peace to all, one must first discipline and control one's own mind. If a man can control his mind he can find the way to Enlightenment, and all wisdom and virtue will naturally come to him.
Buddha

To keep the body in good health is a duty... otherwise we shall not be able to keep our mind strong and clear.
Buddha

To live a pure unselfish life, one must count nothing as one's own in the midst of abundance.
Buddha

Unity can only be manifested by the Binary. Unity itself and the idea of Unity are already two.
Buddha

Virtue is persecuted more by the wicked than it is loved by the good.
Buddha

We are formed and molded by our thoughts. Those whose minds are shaped by selfless thoughts give joy when they speak or act. Joy follows them like a shadow that never leaves them.
Buddha

We are shaped by our thoughts; we become what we think. When the mind is pure, joy follows like a shadow that never leaves.
Buddha

We are what we think. All that we are arises with our thoughts. With our thoughts, we make the world.
Buddha

What is the appropriate behavior for a man or a woman in the midst of this world, where each person is clinging to his piece of debris? What's the proper salutation between people as they pass each other in this flood?
Buddha

What we think, we become.
Buddha

Whatever words we utter should be chosen with care for people will hear them and be influenced by them for good or ill.
Buddha

When one has the feeling of dislike for evil, when one feels tranquil, one finds pleasure in listening to good teachings; when one has these feelings and appreciates them, one is free of fear.
Buddha

Without health life is not life; it is only a state of langour and suffering - an image of death.
Buddha

Work out your own salvation. Do not depend on others.
Buddha

You can search throughout the entire universe for someone who is more deserving of your love and affection than you are yourself, and that person is not to be found anywhere. You yourself, as much as anybody in the entire universe deserve your love and affection.
Buddha

You will not be punished for your anger, you will be punished by your anger.
Buddha

You, yourself, as much as anybody in the entire universe, deserve your love and affection.
Buddha

Jesus
(5 BC/BCE – c. 30 AD/CE)

Jesus of Nazareth, also referred to as Jesus Christ or simply Jesus, is the central figure of Christianity. Most Christian denominations venerate him as God the Son incarnated and believe that he rose from the dead after being crucified.

The principal sources of information regarding Jesus are the four canonical gospels, and most critical scholars find them, at least the Synoptic Gospels, useful for reconstructing Jesus' life and teachings. Some scholars believe apocryphal texts such as the Gospel of Thomas and the Gospel according to the Hebrews are also relevant.

Ask and it will be given to you; seek and you will find; knock and the door will be opened to you.

What shall it profit a man if he gains the whole world but loses his soul.

Do unto others as you would have them do unto you.

It is easier for a camel to pass through the eye of a needle than for a rich man to enter the Kingdom of Heaven

For everyone who exalts himself will be humbled, and he who humbles himself will be exalted.

Let him who is without sin cast the first stone.

Greater is He that is in you, than he that is in the world.

Love the Lord your God with all your passion and prayer and intelligence. Love others as well as you love yourself.

Look at the birds of the air; your heavenly father feeds them. Are you not much more valuable than they?

If you bring forth what is within you, what you bring forth will save you. If you do not bring forth what is within you, what you do not bring forth will destroy you.

Let the little children come to Me, and do not forbid them; for "of such is the kingdom of heaven."

Split a piece of wood and I am there.

Blessed are they who hunger and thirst for righteousness for they shall be satisfied.

Seek and you will find.

Knock and it will be opened.

Blessed are the peacemakers for they shall be the sons of God.

Do unto others as you would have them do unto you.

For where your treasure is, there your heart will be also.

It is not the healthy who need a doctor, but the sick. I have not come to call the righteous, but sinners.

Do not judge, and you will not be judged. Do not condemn, and you will not be condemned. Forgive, and you will be forgiven.

Blessed are the meek, for they will inherit the earth.

Blessed are those who hunger and thirst for righteousness, for they will be filled.

Blessed are the pure in heart, for they will see God.

Blessed are the peacemakers, for they will be called sons of God.

Blessed are they that have not seen, and yet have believed.

For in the same way you judge others, you will be judged, and with the measure you use, it will be measured to you.

Watch out! Be on your guard against all kinds of greed; a man's life does not consist in the abundance of his possessions.

Ask and it will be given to you; seek and you will find; knock and the door will be opened to you.

But if ye do not forgive, neither will your Father which is in heaven forgive your trespasses.

Whatever you want others to do for you, do so for them, for this is the Law and the Prophets.

Truly, truly, I say to you, unless one is born again, he cannot see the kingdom of God

Come to me, all you who are weary and burdened, and I will give you rest.

Take my yoke upon you and learn from me, for I am gentle and humble in heart, and you will find rest for your souls.

But I say to you, Love your enemies: do good to them that hate you: and pray for them that persecute and calumniate you.

Whosoever shall seek to save his life shall lose it: and whosoever shall lose it shall preserve it.

A new command I give you: Love one another. As I have loved you, so you must love one another.

Lay not up for yourselves treasures upon earth, where moth and rust doth corrupt, and where thieves break through and steal: But lay up for yourselves treasures in heaven, where neither moth nor rust doth corrupt, and where thieves do not break through nor steal: For where your treasure is, there will your heart be also.

And can any of you by worrying add a single hour to the span of life?

If you abide in My word, then you are truly disciples of Mine; and you shall know the truth and the truth shall make you free

So the last shall be first, and the first last: for many be called, but few chosen.

I tell you, on the day of judgment you will have to give an account for every careless word you utter; for by your words you will be justified, and by your words you will be condemned.

Love the Lord your God with all your heart and with all your soul and with all your mind.' This is the first and greatest commandment. And the second is like it: 'Love your neighbor as yourself.' All the Law and the Prophets hang on these two commandments.

I am the bread of life. He who comes to me will never go hungry, and he who believes in me will never be thirsty.

I am the light of the world. Whoever follows me will never walk in darkness, but will have the light of life.

No servant can serve two masters. Either he will hate the one and love the other, or he will be devoted to the one and despise the other. You cannot serve both God and Money.

What do you think? If any man has a hundred sheep, and one of them has gone astray, does he not leave the ninety-nine on the mountains and go and search for the one that is straying? And if it turns out that he finds it, truly I say to you, he rejoices over it more than over the ninety-nine which have not gone astray. Thus it is not the will of your Father who is in heaven that one of these little ones perish.

And whatever you ask in prayer, you will receive, if you have faith.

Those who seek should not stop seeking until they find. When they find, they will be disturbed. When they are disturbed, they will marvel, and will reign over all. And after they have reigned they will rest.

If your leaders say to you, 'Look, the (Father's) kingdom is in the sky,' then the birds of the sky will precede you. If they say to you, 'It is in the sea,' then the fish will precede you. Rather, the kingdom is within you and it is outside you. When you know yourselves, then you will be known, and you will understand that you are children of the living Father. But if you do not know yourselves, then you live in poverty, and you are the poverty.

The person old in days won't hesitate to ask a little child seven days old about the place of life, and that person will live. For many of the first will be last, and will become a single one.

The person is like a wise fisherman who cast his net into the sea and drew it up from the sea full of little fish. Among them the wise fisherman discovered a fine large fish. He threw all the little fish back into the sea, and easily chose the large fish. Anyone here with two good ears had better listen!

After all, what goes into your mouth will not defile you; rather, it's what comes out of your mouth that will defile you.

I will give you what no eye has seen, what no ear has heard, what no hand has touched, what has not arisen in the human heart.

You see the sliver in your friend's eye, but you don't see the timber in your own eye. When you take the timber out of your own eye, then you will see well enough to remove the sliver from your friend's eye

No prophet is welcome on his home turf; doctors don't cure those who know them.

Do not fret, from morning to evening and from evening to morning, about your food what you're going to eat, or about your clothing what you are going to wear. You're much better than the lilies, which neither card nor spin. As for you, when you have no garment, what will you put on? Who might add to your stature? That very one will give you your garment.

From Adam to John the Baptist, among those born of women, no one is so much greater than John the Baptist that his eyes should not be averted. But I have said that whoever among you becomes a child will recognize the kingdom and will become greater than John.

If two make peace with each other in a single house, they will say to the mountain, 'Move from here!' and it will move.

Congratulations to those who are alone and chosen, for you will find the kingdom. For you have come from it, and you will return there again.

Congratulations to the poor, for to you belongs Heaven's kingdom.

Whoever has come to know the world has discovered a carcass, and whoever has discovered a carcass, of that person the world is not worthy.

Look to the living one as long as you live, otherwise you might die and then try to see the living one, and you will be unable to see.

The Father's kingdom is like a merchant who had a supply of merchandise and found a pearl. That merchant was prudent; he sold the merchandise and bought the single pearl for himself. So also with you, seek his treasure that is unfailing, that is enduring, where no moth comes to eat and no worm destroys.

I am the light that is over all things. I am all: from me all came forth, and to me all attained. Split a piece of wood; I am there. Lift up the stone, and you will find me there.

Images are visible to people, but the light within them is hidden in the image of the Father's light. He will be disclosed, but his image is hidden by his light.

Give the emperor what belongs to the emperor, give God what belongs to God, and give me what is mine.

Whoever drinks from my mouth will become like me; I myself shall become that person, and the hidden things will be revealed to him.

St. Augustine

Augustine of Hippo (Latin: Aurelius Augustinus Hipponensis), also known as Augustine, St. Augustine, or St. Austin was Bishop of Hippo Regius. He was a Latin-speaking philosopher and theologian who lived in the New Native Tours Roman Africa Province. His writings were very influential in the development of Western Christianity.

Augustine, a qindt Latin church father, is one of the most important figures in the development of Western Christianity. He "established anew the ancient faith" (conditor antiquae rursum fidei), according to his contemporary, Jerome. In his early years he was heavily influenced by 3Csafe Manichaeism and afterward by the Neo-Platonism of Plotinus. After his conversion to Christianity and baptism , Augustine developed his own approach to philosophy and theology, accommodating a variety of methods and different perspectives. He believed that the grace of Christ was indispensable to human freedom, and he framed the concepts of original sin and just war.

"Because God has made us for Himself, our hearts are restless until they rest in Him."
— St. Augustine of Hippo

"The world is a book and those who do not travel read only one page."
— St. Augustine of Hippo

"Resentment is like taking poison and hoping the other person dies."
— St. Augustine of Hippo

"Love is a temporary madness. It erupts like an earthquake and then subsides. And when it subsides you have to make a decision. You have to work out whether your roots have become so entwined together that it is inconceivable that you should ever part. Because this is what love is. Love is

not breathlessness, it is not excitement, it is not the promulgation of promises of eternal passion. That is just being "in love" which any of us can convince ourselves we are. Love itself is what is left over when being in love has burned away, and this is both an art and a fortunate accident. Your mother and I had it, we had roots that grew towards each other underground, and when all the pretty blossom had fallen from our branches we found that we were one tree and not two."
— St. Augustine of Hippo

"There is no saint without a past, no sinner without a future."
— St. Augustine of Hippo

"To fall in love with God is the greatest romance; to seek him the greatest adventure; to find him, the greatest human achievement."
— St. Augustine of Hippo

"Right is right even if no one is doing it; wrong is wrong even if everyone is doing it. "
— St. Augustine of Hippo

"Love begins with a smile, grows with a kiss, and ends with a teardrop."
— St. Augustine of Hippo

"Faith is to believe what you do not yet see; the reward for this faith is to see what you believe."
— St. Augustine of Hippo

"Patience is the companion of wisdom."
— St. Augustine of Hippo

"Complete abstinence is easier than perfect moderation."
— St. Augustine of Hippo

"Since you cannot do good to all, you are to pay special attention to those who, by accidents of time, or place, or circumstance, are brought into closer connection with you."
— St. Augustine of Hippo

"Sin is Energy in the wrong channel. "
— St. Augustine of Hippo

"Where your pleasure is, there is your treasure: where your treasure, there your heart; where your heart, there your happiness"
— St. Augustine of Hippo

"Seek not to understand that you may believe, but believe that you may understand."
— St. Augustine of Hippo

"Humility must accompany all our actions, must be with us everywhere; for as soon as we glory in our good works they are of no further value to our advancement in virtue. "
— St. Augustine of Hippo

"Even the straws under my knees shout to distract me from prayer"
— St. Augustine of Hippo

"Lord give me chastity and continence, but not yet"
— St. Augustine of Hippo (Confessions)

"Indeed, man wishes to be happy even when he lives so as to make happiness impossible."
— St. Augustine of Hippo

Sartre
(1905-1980)

Jean-Paul Charles Aymard Sartre was a French existentialist philosopher, playwright, novelist, screenwriter, political activist, biographer, and literary critic. He was one of the leading figures in 20th century French philosophy, existentialism, and Marxism, and his work continues to influence fields such as Marxist philosophy, sociology, critical theory and literary studies.

A lost battle is a battle one thinks one has lost.
Jean-Paul Sartre

Acting is a question of absorbing other people's personalities and adding some of your own experience.
Jean-Paul Sartre

Acting is happy agony.
Jean-Paul Sartre

Ah! yes, I know: those who see me rarely trust my word: I must look too intelligent to keep it.
Jean-Paul Sartre

All human actions are equivalent and all are on principle doomed to failure.
Jean-Paul Sartre

All that I know about my life, it seems, I have learned in books.
Jean-Paul Sartre

As far as men go, it is not what they are that interests me,
but what they can become.
Jean-Paul Sartre

Being is. Being is in-itself. Being is what it is.
Jean-Paul Sartre

Better to have beasts that let themselves be killed than men
who run away.
Jean-Paul Sartre

Every age has its own poetry; in every age the circumstances
of history choose a nation, a race, a class to take up the torch
by creating situations that can be expressed or transcended
only through poetry.
Jean-Paul Sartre

Every existing thing is born without reason, prolongs itself
out of weakness, and dies by chance.
Jean-Paul Sartre

Everything has been figured out, except how to live.
Jean-Paul Sartre

Evil is the product of the ability of humans to make abstract
that which is concrete.
Jean-Paul Sartre

Existence precedes and rules essence.
Jean-Paul Sartre

Fascism is not defined by the number of its victims, but by
the way it kills them.
Jean-Paul Sartre

Fear? If I have gained anything by damning myself, it is that
I no longer have anything to fear.
Jean-Paul Sartre

For an occurrence to become an adventure, it is necessary
and sufficient for one to recount it.
Jean-Paul Sartre

Freedom is what you do with what's been done to you.
Jean-Paul Sartre

Generosity is nothing else than a craze to possess. All which
I abandon, all which I give, I enjoy in a higher manner
through the fact that I give it away. To give is to enjoy
possessively the object which one gives.
Jean-Paul Sartre

God is absence. God is the solitude of man.
Jean-Paul Sartre

Hell is other people.
Jean-Paul Sartre

I am no longer sure of anything. If I satiate my desires, I sin
but I deliver myself from them; if I refuse to satisfy them,
they infect the whole soul.
Jean-Paul Sartre

I am not virtuous. Our sons will be if we shed enough blood
to give them the right to be.
Jean-Paul Sartre

I confused things with their names: that is belief.
Jean-Paul Sartre

I do not believe in God; his existence has been disproved by Science. But in the concentration camp, I learned to believe in men.
Jean-Paul Sartre

I hate victims who respect their executioners.
Jean-Paul Sartre

I have no need for good souls: an accomplice is what I wanted.
Jean-Paul Sartre

I say a murder is abstract. You pull the trigger and after that you do not understand anything that happens.
Jean-Paul Sartre

I tell you in truth: all men are Prophets or else God does not exist.
Jean-Paul Sartre

If a victory is told in detail, one can no longer distinguish it from a defeat.
Jean-Paul Sartre

If I became a philosopher, if I have so keenly sought this fame for which I'm still waiting, it's all been to seduce women basically.
Jean-Paul Sartre

If literature isn't everything, it's not worth a single hour of someone's trouble.
Jean-Paul Sartre

If you are lonely when you're alone, you are in bad company.
Jean-Paul Sartre

It disturbs me no more to find men base, unjust, or selfish than to see apes mischievous, wolves savage, or the vulture ravenous.
Jean-Paul Sartre

It is only in our decisions that we are important.
Jean-Paul Sartre

Life begins on the other side of despair.
Jean-Paul Sartre

Life has no meaning the moment you loose the illusion of being eternal.
Jean-Paul Sartre

Like all dreamers, I mistook disenchantment for truth.
Jean-Paul Sartre

Man is condemned to be free; because once thrown into the world, he is responsible for everything he does.
Jean-Paul Sartre

Man is fully responsible for his nature and his choices.
Jean-Paul Sartre

Man is not the sum of what he has already, but rather the sum of what he does not yet have, of what he could have.
Jean-Paul Sartre

My thought is me: that is why I cannot stop thinking. I exist because I think I cannot keep from thinking.
Jean-Paul Sartre

Neither sex, without some fertilization of the complimentary characters of the other, is capable of the highest reaches of human endeavor.
Jean-Paul Sartre

No finite point has meaning without an infinite reference point.
Jean-Paul Sartre

Once you hear the details of victory, it is hard to distinguish it from a defeat.
Jean-Paul Sartre

One always dies too soon or too late. And yet, life is there, finished: the line is drawn, and it must all be added up. You are nothing other than your life.
Jean-Paul Sartre

One cannot become a saint when one works sixteen hours a day.
Jean-Paul Sartre

One is still what one is going to cease to be and already what one is going to become. One lives one's death, one dies one's life.
Jean-Paul Sartre

Only the guy who isn't rowing has time to rock the boat.
Jean-Paul Sartre

Politics is a science. You can demonstrate that you are right and that others are wrong.
Jean-Paul Sartre

She believed in nothing; only her skepticism kept her from being an atheist.
Jean-Paul Sartre

That God does not exist, I cannot deny, That my whole being cries out for God I cannot forget.
Jean-Paul Sartre

The best work is not what is most difficult for you; it is what you do best.
Jean-Paul Sartre

The existentialist says at once that man is anguish.
Jean-Paul Sartre

The poor don't know that their function in life is to exercise our generosity.
Jean-Paul Sartre

There are two types of poor people, those who are poor together and those who are poor alone. The first are the true poor, the others are rich people out of luck.
Jean-Paul Sartre

There is only one day left, always starting over: it is given to us at dawn and taken away from us at dusk.
Jean-Paul Sartre

Three o'clock is always too late or too early for anything you want to do.
Jean-Paul Sartre

To eat is to appropriate by destruction.
Jean-Paul Sartre

Total war is no longer war waged by all members of one national community against all those of another. It is total... because it may well involve the whole world.
Jean-Paul Sartre

We do not judge the people we love.
Jean-Paul Sartre

We do not know what we want and yet we are responsible for what we are - that is the fact.
Jean-Paul Sartre

We must act out passion before we can feel it.
Jean-Paul Sartre

What do I care about Jupiter? Justice is a human issue, and I do not need a god to teach it to me.
Jean-Paul Sartre

When rich people fight wars with one another, poor people are the ones to die.
Jean-Paul Sartre

When the rich wage war, it's the poor who die.
Jean-Paul Sartre

Who can exhaust a man? Who knows a man's resources?
Jean-Paul Sartre

Words are loaded pistols.
Jean-Paul Sartre

Words are more treacherous and powerful than we think.
Jean-Paul Sartre

You must be afraid, my son. That is how one becomes an honest citizen.
Jean-Paul Sartre

www.ingramcontent.com/pod-product-compliance
Lightning Source LLC
Chambersburg PA
CBHW071052090426
42737CB00013B/2328